America's Favorite Drug: Coffee and Your Health

Bonnie Edwards, RN

*With a foreword by
Mark Wexman, MD
and Karen Wexman, MD*

ODONIAN PRESS
BERKELEY, CALIFORNIA

Additional copies of this and other Odonian books are available for $5 + $2 shipping per *order* (not per *book*) from Odonian Press, Box 7776, Berkeley CA 94707. Please write for information on quantity discounts, or call us at 510 524 3143. Distribution to book stores and wholesalers is through Publishers Group West, Box 8843, Emeryville CA 94662, 510 658 3453 (toll-free: 800 788 3123).

Editors: Janet Reed, John Kadyk, Christine Carswell

Inside design, page layout, production:
Karen Faria, Arthur Naiman

Cover design: Arthur Naiman, John Miller/Big Fish

Cover painting: Trevor Irvin

Printing: Michelle Selby, Jim Puzey /
Consolidated Printers, Berkeley, California

Series editor: Arthur Naiman

Series coordinator: Susan McCallister

Edwards, Bonnie, 1948–
America's favorite drug : coffee and your health / Bonnie Edwards.
   p.   cm.
Includes bibliographical references (p.   )
ISBN 1-878825-50-X : $5.00
1. Coffee—Health aspects. I. Title.
QP801.C24E38 1992
613.3—dc20

92-3272
CIP

Printed in the United States of America First printing, August 1992

To my mother, Patricia,
with gratitude for teaching me
humor and playfulness,
two of her most valuable gifts

and

to my mentor, Ruth Ross,
with gratitude for her loving guidance

Odonian Press gets its name from Ursula Le Guin's wonderful novel The Dispossessed (though we have no connection with Ms. Le Guin or any of her publishers). The last story in her collection The Wind's Twelve Quarters also features the Odonians.

Odonian Press donates at least 10% (last year it was 36%) of its aftertax income to organizations working for social justice.

Contents

Foreword

America is a country of coffee drinkers. Most of us have childhood memories of that marvelous aroma of freshly perked java in the air. Our initial encounter with coffee may have been a bitter disappointment, but now we savor the last drop.

The tradition of a cup of coffee (or two, or three, or more) may be affecting you more than you realize. Its possible negative and positive consequences are thoroughly discussed in this book.

Bonnie Edwards has sifted the beans of available research, percolated them through the filter of her knowledge and awareness and has given us a full cup of interesting facts, still-unanswered questions and useful recommendations.

She respects your intelligence and your ability to review the facts and make informed decisions. Whether you're concerned with coffee and pregnancy, heart disease, cancer, headaches or sleep disturbance, her presentation of the controversies is clear and well researched.

What we eat and drink contributes significantly to our health (and to today's skyrocketing health care costs). This book provides a basis for moving from addiction and habit to conscious choice in determining your coffee consumption.

Mark Wexman, MD
Assistant Professor of Medicine, UCSF;
Cardiologist, Marin General Hospital

Karen Wexman, MD
Internist, Marin County, California

Acknowledgments

I'm very grateful to the librarians at Planetree Health Resource Center in San Francisco and at the UCSF Medical Center Library for the valuable assistance given me in locating information and doing computer searches. The librarians at the Corte Madera and the Marin Civic Center libraries were also extremely helpful.

Many thanks to my friend, Caryn Papiro, RPT, for doing a preliminary edit of my early work and giving very valuable input. I was very happy with the editing assistance provided by Janet Reed. Warm thanks to John Kadyk for his thoughtful attention to detail.

Many thanks to my employers, UCSF Prenatal Diagnosis and William Baeza Chiropractic, for giving me flexibility in my work schedule and the needed time off to complete the book. Warm thanks to all my supportive co-workers.

I'm extremely grateful for the support and encouragement of my loving friends: Jacki Annes, Lawrence Atencio, Lou Caires, Bruce Edwards, Percy Edwards, Pauline France, Marcy Ann Marie Fraser, Karen Gilbert, Laura Lesley Gilbert, Beth Kershaw, Mark Marigo, my sister Patty Mathison, Mary Jo McMann, Marijana Stipanov and Tim Tomashek. Last but not least, I'd like to thank my publisher, Arthur Naiman, who is one of the most caring, supportive and generous men I know.

Introduction

Relax! This book isn't out to get you to give up coffee. Rather, it's to help you be aware of how coffee affects you, and how it can damage—or even improve—your health. After reading this book, some of you may continue your coffee-drinking habits. Others, however, may decide to make changes.

Americans drink more than 400 million cups of coffee daily. Over half the population drinks at least two cups a day. 25% of coffee-drinkers consume about five cups daily, and another 25% drink ten or more cups a day. Coffee has become part of our social life. When we take a break with a co-worker, it's a "coffee break." When we get together with a friend, it's often "for coffee."

But coffee isn't just a drink—it's a drug. Hundreds of thousands of law-abiding citizens are physically addicted to coffee because of its caffeine punch. In fact, more people in the US are addicted to coffee than to any other drug—it's more popular than alcohol, tobacco or marijuana. Because it's so widely used, coffee has the potential to affect the health of millions of people.

"OK," you may be asking, "why is she picking on coffee? What about other sources of caffeine like tea and colas?" The fact is that coffee contains more caffeine than tea or colas, and most Americans get their caffeine from coffee.

7

Aside from caffeine, coffee contains literally hundreds of other chemicals that aren't found in teas or caffeinated soft drinks. With that many chemicals, it's inevitable some will be bad for you. And, indeed, some are known carcinogens.

I was a coffee addict. I was compulsive about having two or three caffè lattes daily, as well as several cups of strong coffee. I had developed some tolerance to the drug so that I had to drink more and more to get the effect I wanted. But like most people, probably, I didn't know how addicted I was (and how it was affecting my health) until I stopped— and realized how much better I felt.

So if you're a coffee addict too, I understand how you feel. It smells so good, it tastes so good and it gives you such a boost—at least for a while. I know how hard it is to give it up, and that you won't want to.

But maybe you will. Or maybe you'll prefer to cut back to a moderate one or two cups a day. Before you decide, you should know the many ways that coffee can affect you. Some you may have suspected; others may surprise you.

Each chapter begins with a general discussion of a potential health concern. That's followed by a list of what research has discovered about coffee and that area of concern. Finally, I suggest some things you can do to minimize your risk.

Anxiety

About anxiety and panic attacks

Anxiety is the most common mental health problem in the United States. About thirteen million Americans suffer from some kind of anxiety disorder, including panic attacks. A panic attack can start with increased heart rate, heart palpitations, jitters, anxiety, irritability, sweating and rapid breathing.

Many people take tranquilizers to help them cope with day-to-day stress, controlling their symptoms but not getting rid of the underlying problem.

What research has discovered

- *Adrenaline*, a hormone that the adrenal glands release in response to stress or fear, increases the rate and force of the heartbeat and can cause restlessness and nervousness. Human studies have found that caffeine combined with emotional stress raises adrenaline levels more than either caffeine or emotional stress alone.

- Caffeine interferes with *adenosine*, a brain chemical that normally has a calming effect. This increases nerve activity.

9

- Studies on humans have shown that caffeine increases brainwave activity, and studies of animal brains have shown what specific areas are stimulated—those associated with sensations, primitive behavior and emotion. So caffeine is likely to make people more emotionally volatile and predisposed to anxiety.

- Caffeine can also cause muscle tension. For example, a study of psychiatric patients showed a link between coffee drinking and "restless legs"—a common condition that can be caused by anxiety or mineral deficiencies.

- Since caffeine can bring on the physiological symptoms of anxiety, coffee drinkers may be misdiagnosed with anxiety disorders when they're actually suffering from *caffeinism* (the syndrome associated with heavy caffeine intake). As a result, they may be subjected to expensive and unnecessary physical exams, or given tranquilizers they don't need.

  One researcher reviewed the charts of 100 randomly chosen psychiatric outpatients. He found that although 42% of these people had complained of anxiety, none of their health-care providers had ever questioned them about their coffee- or tea-drinking habits.

- If you already have a problem with anxiety, coffee can aggravate it. In one study, the caffeine in four cups of coffee sharply raised the level of *lactate*—an enzyme known to produce panic attacks—in the blood of people with panic disorders. In fact, as few as one or two cups can provoke a panic attack in someone who's prone to them.

📭 Some evidence indicates that caffeine decreases the effectiveness of sedatives and tranquilizers, which are often pre-scribed for anxiety disorders.

What you can do

📭 If any of the following apply to you, you may want to cut back on coffee, eliminate it (permanently or temporarily) or switch to decaf: coffee makes you jittery and nervous; you're having emotional prob-lems; you're going through some stress-ful life transitions; or you have a history of an anxiety or panic disorder.

📭 Even if your doctor believes that some-thing other than coffee drinking is caus-ing your anxiety and has prescribed a sedative or tranquilizer for you, switching to decaf will make certain that caffeine doesn't counter the medication's effect.

📭 If you decide to cut back or quit, you may find that caffeine withdrawal actu-ally makes you *more* anxious for a while. For tips on avoiding that, see the chapter on cutting back or quitting at the back of the book.

Asthma

About asthma

Asthma usually begins in childhood, but can develop at any age. It's becoming more common in the United States and in other industrialized nations. About twelve million people in the US—one out of every twenty—suffer from asthma.

People with asthma are often hypersensitive to *allergens* (substances that cause allergic reactions, like dust, pollen, feathers, animal hair, environmental pollutants and certain foods). Cold air, heavy physical exertion, emotional stress and certain drugs (especially aspirin) can also bring on an asthma attack.

When an asthmatic person has an attack, spasms occur in the smaller airways (*bronchioles*) of the lungs. This causes breathlessness, coughing, wheezing, tightness in the chest and increased mucous production in the lungs.

One oral medication commonly used to prevent asthma attacks is *theophylline*. It's also used to stimulate breathing in premature babies (who commonly have episodes of *apnea*—times when their breathing stops). Theophylline is manufactured from caffeine extracted from coffee and tea, but is considered more effective than caffeine itself. Theophylline treatment must be monitored closely, though, as it can have adverse effects.

What research has discovered

- Caffeine helps relieve asthma symptoms by relaxing the smooth muscle in the airways of the lungs, allowing them to expand. The caffeine in three cups of coffee can significantly raise the levels of *epinephrine* and *norepinephrine* in the blood, which bring about this effect. Caffeine can also increase the rate and depth of breathing.

- In one study, coffee was found to be just as effective as theophylline in relieving asthma symptoms. Some doctors have suggested that, in an emergency situation where asthma drugs aren't available, two to three cups of strong coffee may serve as a good substitute.

- A survey of 72,000 people in Italy found that one cup of coffee a day reduced the occurrence of asthma symptoms by 5%, and three or more cups reduced them by 30%. Unfortunately, the researchers didn't find out what kind of coffee the participants were drinking, and some Italian coffees contain up to 50% more caffeine than others; so we don't know exactly how much caffeine these cup-per-day figures actually represent.

■ Theophylline and caffeine taken together can cause severe nervousness, sleep disturbance, stomach upset and, in extreme cases, seizures.

What you can do

■ If you have asthma, are caught somewhere without your medications and begin to have an attack, drink two or three cups of strong coffee right away.

■ If you have asthma and aren't taking prescription medications on a regular basis, drinking coffee every day may help prevent symptoms. But then you'll have to deal with the various side effects of coffee described elsewhere in this book.

■ If you're taking theophylline, avoid regular coffee—the two combined can make you a nervous wreck.

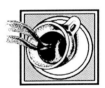

Blood pressure

About blood pressure

Blood pressure is the force blood exerts against the walls of your arteries as it flows through them. High blood pressure (also called *hypertension*) is a concern because it means that the heart and blood vessels are working under strained conditions. Anything that elevates blood pressure should be considered potentially dangerous.

Two measurements make up a blood pressure reading: the first is taken during the surge of blood as the heart contracts (*systolic pressure*); the second is taken between heartbeats (*diastolic pressure*). Since blood pressure normally goes up in response to stress and physical activity, it's always measured while the person is at rest.

Normal blood pressure for young, healthy adults averages 115/75 or 120/80. These numbers tend to increase with age—130/90 would be considered normal when you're 60. Hypertension is usually defined as a blood pressure of 140/90 or higher.

High blood pressure is a common malady: Sixty million Americans have it, and 300,000 die each year from its complications. If untreated, it can lead to heart, kidney and eye problems, and increases the risk of stroke. Health-care providers prescribe weight loss, low salt diets, exercise and antihypertensive drugs in an attempt to bring blood pressure down.

What research has discovered

■ Caffeine's been shown to increase blood pressure significantly in those who don't habitually use it. The maximum effect occurs fifteen to ninety minutes after consumption, and it can take three or four hours for blood pressure to return to normal.

■ Since caffeine tolerance develops after a few days of regular consumption, coffee has little effect on the blood pressure of the habitual coffee drinker whose blood pressure is otherwise normal.

But coffee does affect the blood pressure of the habitual coffee drinker whose blood pressure is already above normal. A study of mildly hypertensive people who drank coffee regularly showed that their first cup of the day significantly raised their blood pressure. So coffee seems to exacerbate the symptoms of those who already have hypertension, but more studies are needed to confirm this.

■ The caffeine in three cups of coffee will raise your production of cortisol, a stress hormone. Cortisol causes the blood vessels to constrict and the heart to pump harder (which leads to higher blood pressure).

This may explain why caffeine combined with stress increases blood pressure more than the stress would by itself. The stress can be mental, emotional or even physical, like strenuous exercise.

- People with family histories of high blood pressure are genetically more prone to rising blood pressure when stress and caffeine are combined. One study found that people who had a parent that suffered from hypertension had a greater increase in cortisol and blood pressure when they consumed caffeine under stress than those with no family history of hypertension.

- People with family histories of high blood pressure tend to have a significant increase in blood pressure when they exercise. Having caffeine beforehand increases it even more, making the combination of coffee and exercise particularly hazardous for such people.

- Caffeine can nullify the beneficial effects of medications taken for high blood pressure, making expensive drugs useless.

- Some diet pills and cold medicines (like Contac and Alka Seltzer Plus) contain *phenylpropanolamine*, which can increase blood pressure—to the point of causing strokes in research animals. Drinking three to five cups of coffee after taking one of these pills has been found to increase blood pressure more than either the pill or coffee alone, significantly increasing the risk of stroke.

■ Birth-control pills both raise women's blood pressure and prolong exposure to caffeine (by decreasing the rate at which it's *metabolized*, or broken down for use by the body). So combining birth-control pills with coffee is likely to raise blood pressure more than either the pill or caffeine separately.

■ Some evidence indicates that a variety of antidepressant medication known as *MAO (monoamine oxidase)-inhibitors* may cause increased blood pressure if taken with caffeine. Marplan (Isocarboxazid), Nardil (Phenelzine), Niamid (Nialamide) and Parnate (Tranylcypromine) are commonly-used drugs of this type.

What you can do

■ If you drink coffee habitually and aren't in any way at risk for high blood pressure, there's no evidence that continuing to drink coffee will raise your blood pressure.

■ If you have high blood pressure or are at risk for it, either eliminate coffee from your diet, keep your consumption down to one or two cups a day or switch to decaf.

■ If you're under a lot of stress, limit your coffee intake or switch to decaf.

■ If you have a family history of high blood pressure, don't drink coffee before exercising.

■ If you're taking birth-control pills, medication for high blood pressure, or an MAO-inhibiting antidepressant, don't drink caffeinated coffee.

■ If you're taking diet pills or cold medications containing phenylpropanolamine, avoid coffee and other sources of caffeine for several hours before and after taking them. If you're taking these medications all day long, stick to decaf or avoid coffee altogether.

■ Very low blood pressure can also be a problem. Those who have it often experience dizziness when getting up from a seated or prone position, and may even pass out as a result. If you have this problem, drinking a couple of cups of coffee in the morning may help.

Breast-feeding

About breast-feeding

Breast-feeding has made a comeback in recent years in the United States. It's the most natural way for a mother to feed her baby and is now considered by many experts to be more healthful than formula.

Breast milk is the most ideally balanced food for newborns. Besides nutrients, it provides them with valuable antibodies they haven't formed on their own, giving them added protection against disease.

Many American women are very cautious about what they eat and drink during pregnancy, but are less so once their babies have been born. But food, drugs and even environmental pollutants can be passed to the baby through breast milk, just as they're passed to the fetus in the womb.

So if you drink coffee while you're breast-feeding, your baby is effectively drinking coffee too—and becoming addicted to it. The consequences for newborns are particularly harsh since they haven't developed the liver enzymes (proteins that catalyze biochemical reactions) necessary to break down drugs and toxins.

What research has discovered

◗ Babies whose mothers drink coffee during pregnancy can become addicted to caffeine before birth. If these babies aren't breast-fed after birth, they'll miss their caffeine supply.

Some researchers think some bottle-fed newborns develop breathing problems because they're going through caffeine withdrawal. Breast-fed newborns whose mothers continue drinking coffee don't go through withdrawal.

◗ If a woman abstains from drinking coffee during pregnancy, but then starts again while breast-feeding, her baby may have a stronger caffeine reaction (often colic, jitters and fussiness) than a baby exposed to caffeine before birth. Researchers have found this stronger reaction even in older children.

◗ Newborns can't metabolize caffeine, so they have to excrete it in their urine. This is a much slower process than metabolizing it, so the caffeine remains in their bodies longer than it does in adults—sometimes three to four days—stimulating the baby's nervous system that entire time.

◗ Some evidence indicates that breast-fed babies whose mothers drink a lot of coffee may be especially irritable and sleep poorly.

- According to some research, the babies of nursing mothers who drink six to eight cups of coffee a day may gain weight more slowly.

What you can do

- If you're wondering why your baby is keeping you up all night, consider how much coffee you've been drinking. Try eliminating it, cutting back or switching to decaf. (If you drank coffee during pregnancy, reduce your intake gradually to wean your baby off the caffeine.)

- If your baby suffers from colic, your coffee drinking might be the culprit. Eliminate all coffee, including decaf (which also causes digestive upset) for a few weeks and see if there's a change in your baby's behavior. (But cut back gradually if you drank coffee during pregnancy.)

Cancer

About cancer

Cancer is the second most common cause of death in the United States, after heart disease. For the most part, it's a disease of age: for each decade after 30 years of age, the risk of developing cancer doubles. Maybe one of the reasons cancer is more common now is that the nation's population of senior citizens is steadily increasing.

Cancer forms when a *carcinogen* (cancer-causing substance) causes cells to mutate and divide rapidly and uncontrollably. These abnormal cells form tumors and often infiltrate surrounding tissues. This usually destroys tissue and nerves, interrupting the body's normal functions.

Cancer cells can also spread to other parts of the body. The cells continue to divide uncontrollably at these new locations (called *metastases*), forming new tumors.

Interestingly, Mormons and Seventh Day Adventists have extremely low incidences of cancer among their members. Both groups abstain from smoking, alcohol and caffeine. (Smoking and alcohol are both known to increase one's risk of cancer though, so they may account for this difference.)

What research has discovered

◼ Caffeine has been identified as a carcinogen, but it isn't the only one in the coffee we drink, nor the worst. Among the others are creosote, pyrndine and tars, all created by the high heat of roasting—as are the polycylic aromatic hydrocarbons, which produce that wonderful flavor and smell, but are also thought to cause cancer. For this reason, roasted coffee beans are much more carcinogenic than raw ones. The darker the roast, the greater the potential hazard.

◼ Although coffee contains carcinogens, the jury is still out on coffee and cancer. Many, many studies have been done, with varying results. Research done on 16,000 Norwegians, discussed at the Thirteenth International Cancer Conference in 1983, found no link between coffee drinking and cancer in any part of the body. But many other studies have found links.

Unfortunately, few studies have eliminated factors like smoking and high-fat diets from their research populations, which makes their results impossible to evaluate. The fact that such studies have been done in different countries, with varying lifestyles and methods of preparing coffee, makes comparison and evaluation even more complicated.

- Everyone agrees that factors like smoking and alcohol consumption pose much greater cancer risks than coffee drinking.

- Coffee may actually provide some protection against a few types of cancer. Evidence suggests that caffeine slows or inhibits tumor growth in the thyroid, breast, colon and rectum, but it's not known how.

- Most coffee-growing countries allow the use of pesticides which have been banned in the US after they were found to cause cancer in laboratory animals. FDA tests have found traces of several banned pesticides in imported coffee beans.

- Paper coffee filters often contain dioxin, a carcinogen that forms when the paper is bleached. Some of this dioxin can leach into the coffee as it's being filtered.

Research on lab animals indicates that although dioxin may promote tumors, it doesn't appear to cause cancer directly. Studies of dioxin's effect on humans have been inconclusive so far, but the threat doesn't appear significant. The FDA estimated that dioxin from coffee filters would lead to less than one additional case of cancer among a million people over a lifetime.

■ Pancreatic cancer is one of the deadliest kinds, resulting in death 5% more often than lung cancer does.

The first study to show a link between coffee and pancreatic cancer was done at Harvard. Both regular and decaffeinated coffees were implicated, but not tea. This study has been widely criticized (as have others with similar findings) for using a narrow selection of participants and for not taking other factors into consideration. Subsequent studies have produced mixed results, some showing a correlation and others none at all.

Actually, a number of studies have found a stronger link to decaf than to regular coffee—perhaps because, until 1975, the solvent trichlorethylene (TCE) was used to remove caffeine from coffee. TCE was also formerly used by the dry-cleaning industry, where the incidence of pancreatic cancer was found to be higher than in the general population.

The chemical now being used to decaffeinate coffee, methylene chloride, is supposed to be safer, but it's toxic too (for details, see the chapter on decaffeinated coffee at the back of the book).

More work needs to be done to determine whether there really is a link between coffee drinking and pancreatic cancer. The existing data suggests that drinking two or more cups of coffee a day could increase one's risk. But one scientist suggested that it may be the cancer that leads to more coffee drinking, rather than the other way around, because the damaged pancreas brings on more thirst for fluids of any kind, including coffee.

Ovarian cancer is most common in women over 50, but it can occur at any age. It's the fourth leading cause of cancer death among women.

Although some research has shown little evidence of a link between coffee drinking and ovarian cancer, a few studies have produced striking results. One showed no increased risk from drinking one cup of coffee a day, but double the average risk from drinking two or more.

Another study showed a three-and-a-half times greater risk of ovarian cancer for women who had consumed coffee regularly for over 40 years, compared to those who'd never regularly drunk it. This study suggests that how long you've drunk coffee is more important than how much you drink.

- Bladder cancer only accounts for about 4% of all cancers in the United States. It's three times more common in men than women and is most often found in older people, the average age of diagnosis being about 65.

There's some evidence linking coffee drinking and bladder cancer, but most of these studies have been criticized for not factoring out smoking, which by itself doubles one's risk of bladder cancer. Some scientists think coffee may increase the cancer-causing potential of another factor, rather than causing bladder cancer itself.

Some believe that the acids in coffee may irritate sensitive bladders, making them more vulnerable to the disease. One study showed an elevated risk of bladder cancer from drinking more than four cups of coffee a day. But bladder cancer is also linked to drinking over two liters of any fluid a day. So drinking lots of coffee may increase risk simply by adding to the total amount of fluid drunk.

- Kidney cancer is another less common cancer that's been linked with coffee drinking. Coffee stimulates the kidneys, causing increased urination. One study showed that excessive coffee drinking (over seven cups a day) increased the risk of kidney cancer by 30%.

What you can do

- There isn't really enough evidence of a cancer threat to recommend that you quit drinking coffee. But if you're very health-conscious, it can't hurt to limit your drinking to one or two cups a day. (Switching to decaf won't necessarily decrease the risk, since those beans have been roasted too, and therefore contain many of the same carcinogens as regular coffee.)

- Stick to more lightly roasted beans; since roasting creates carcinogens, less roasting means less risk.

- Use only water-processed decaffeinated coffee in order to avoid exposure to methylene chloride.

- Even though dioxin doesn't appear very threatening, to be safe, use unbleached coffee filters or buy a gold-plated filter (which can be reused). In blind taste tests, experts found no taste difference between the coffee from bleached and unbleached filters. They found the quality of coffee from a gold-plated filter to be similar (although a fine sediment remains in gold-filtered coffee).

- If any member of your family has had cancer, you may be at increased cancer risk yourself, depending on the type, since not all forms are hereditary. But since caffeine may inhibit tumor growth in some areas of the body and provoke it in others, you might want to consider what types of cancer you could be more prone to before changing your habits.

For example, if you're a woman who has close female relatives with breast cancer, it may actually be good for you to drink coffee, since caffeine seems to inhibit tumor growth in breast tissue. But you could avoid other potential ill effects of coffee by drinking tea. Tea would provide you with the caffeine without exposing you to the other carcinogens in coffee.

Cholesterol

About cholesterol

An estimated 60 million Americans have high cholesterol, which has been associated with *atherosclerosis* (also known as "hardening of the arteries"). Atherosclerosis is caused by fatty deposits building up on the artery walls.

Although usually a slow process, the development of atherosclerosis can be accelerated by other factors, like high blood pressure or smoking.

In time, atherosclerosis makes the arteries inflexible and narrow, reducing blood flow. Eventually, blood flow may be blocked altogether. If this happens in a heart muscle, part of the heart tissue may die, causing a heart attack. If the blood flow to the brain is blocked, the result will be a stroke.

Heart attacks and strokes are two of the leading causes of death in the United States and other industrialized countries, where the diet is higher in animal fat than in poorer countries. (The body produces cholesterol from animal fat, and absorbs it directly from cholesterol-rich foods like eggs.)

That's why health-care providers urge you to have your blood cholesterol level checked regularly, to get it within the desired range and to keep it under control. If the serum cholesterol level of your blood is found to be over 200, you should take immediate measures to reduce it. A level of 200 or above significantly increases your risk of cardiovascular disease.

What research has discovered

▪ Studies at Stanford and Kaiser Permanente in California, and others elsewhere have found that coffee drinking raises cholesterol levels.

▪ Three studies in Australia also linked coffee consumption to increased cholesterol levels. But in two of the studies, the link appeared in women only. The women who drank two or more cups of coffee a day showed a greater increase than those who had none at all.

▪ Several Norwegian studies have found that heavy coffee drinking may raise blood cholesterol levels significantly—up to 14%—but some say this increase depends on how the coffee was prepared. In Norway, many people make coffee by soaking the grounds in boiling water, the way you might over a campfire. One Norwegian study interviewed 18,000 coffee drinkers; those who prepared their coffee by boiling it had higher cholesterol levels than those who used other methods, like filtering. So the amount of time coffee steeps in hot water may affect how much it raises cholesterol levels.

But these Norwegian studies didn't consider and adjust for factors like smoking or high fat diets, which also affect cholesterol. They also didn't distinguish between those who drank their coffee black and those who used cream. Using cream would, of course, increase one's cholesterol level.

- The amount of increase in cholesterol depends on the amount of coffee consumed as well as how it was prepared. In one Norwegian study involving 14,500 people, cholesterol was 5% higher in those who drank one to four cups a day than in those who didn't drink coffee at all. And it was 14% higher in those who drank nine or more cups a day.

- Caffeine doesn't appear to be the cause of increased cholesterol among coffee drinkers. Tea and cola drinkers haven't shown an increase in cholesterol levels, although very strong black tea can contain almost as much caffeine as coffee. One recent US study suggested that even decaffeinated coffee may raise the level of cholesterol. So it could be one or more of coffee's hundreds of other chemicals that has this effect.

What you can do

- Use a filter method to prepare your coffee. It may be that the filter traps some of whatever it is that raises cholesterol, or that the grounds don't release as much of it as when they're steeped in boiling water.

- If your cholesterol level is within or below normal range and you enjoy having two or three cups of coffee a day, you can probably continue without worrying. A slight increase in cholesterol isn't likely to harm you.

  If you're in that 25% of coffee drinkers who drink ten or more cups a day, you might consider cutting back. You're risking a significant increase in your cholesterol level.

- If you have high cholesterol, you may want to limit your coffee intake to an occasional treat or cut it out altogether (you should also adhere to a low-fat, low-cholesterol diet). If you feel like you can't survive without the caffeine lift, try black tea, which doesn't appear to affect cholesterol.

Digestive disorders

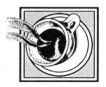

About digestive disorders

The stomach contains digestive juices made up of acid and enzymes that break down food before it goes on to the intestines. The stomach's walls are lined with mucous, which protects the stomach itself from being digested.

Excess stomach acid is a common cause of digestive disorders. If something upsets the pH balance of the digestive fluids, the stomach may produce too much acid. This excess can then cause indigestion by eating away at the mucous lining. If the acid penetrates through the lining to the tissue of the stomach wall itself, it can cause *ulcers*, which are raw, open sores.

Excess stomach acid can also cause ulcers in the *duodenum*, which connects the stomach to the intestine. The reflux of acid from the stomach into the esophagus, which causes heartburn, can cause ulcers there as well.

Ulcers are very common in the United States. One out of every eight people will develop an ulcer at some point in life. And even after an ulcer heals, there's a 50% to 80% chance it will recur.

The prevalence of indigestion, heartburn and ulcers has led to the widespread use of drugs to relieve their symptoms. Antacids relieve indigestion by neutralizing stomach acid, and can help ulcers heal by protecting the stomach lining. Anti-ulcer drugs usually work by either reducing the amount of stomach acid or protecting the ulcer from its action.

What research has discovered

- The caffeine, oils and acids in coffee irritate the stomach lining, which can cause excessive production of stomach acid and lead to a variety of digestive ailments. Decaf, which contains the same oils and acids as regular coffee (plus, if it isn't water-processed, traces of methylene chloride) brings on a similar increase in stomach acid.

  Nausea, bloating, gas, heartburn, diarrhea and ulcers have all been associated with coffee drinking in various studies. But individuals seem to vary widely in their susceptibility to these ailments.

- Drinking coffee on an empty stomach produces an even greater increase in stomach acid, and can bring on stomach pain almost immediately in some people.

- Research has shown a definite link between coffee drinking and ulcers. One large study of 25,000 men showed that those who drink coffee have about a 72% higher risk of developing ulcers than those who don't.

🖤 People who already have ulcers are highly susceptible to coffee's ill effects. When they drink coffee, their digestive juices become more acidic and stay that way longer than others' do.

In one study, when people without ulcers drank three cups of coffee, their stomachs produced 100% more hydrochloric acid than normal. But this effect only lasted an hour and a half. When ulcer patients consumed the same amount, their acid production went up by 150% initially; after two hours, it was still 100% higher than before they'd drunk the coffee.

🖤 Another study, involving 150 ulcer patients, found a strong correlation between the amount of coffee drunk and the severity of ulcerlike symptoms that the patients experienced. The study found that patients would voluntarily drink less coffee based on the digestive discomfort they were experiencing.

🖤 Some anti-ulcer drugs, like cimetidine (Tagamet), slow down the rate at which the body metabolizes caffeine. So not only does coffee defeat their purpose (by increasing stomach acid), these drugs extend caffeine's effects by keeping it in the bloodstream longer.

- Coffee affects the lower esophageal sphincter pressure (which controls the opening between the stomach and throat). Whether the pressure increases or decreases depends on the individual, but researchers think that *any* change in this pressure can cause a reflux of stomach acid into the throat, giving the coffee drinker heartburn. Some physicians think that people who get heartburn this way may already have an abnormality of the sphincter pressure, which coffee exacerbates.

- Coffee tends to slow down the passage of waste through the small intestine and speed it up in the large intestine. This may be what causes the diarrhea that many people get after drinking coffee.

- Some research suggests that it's not just how much coffee you drink, but how long you've been drinking coffee that can cause digestive ills. If you've been drinking coffee for years, the chronic irritation of your stomach lining could lead to inflammation and pain—even if you only drink two cups a day.

What you can do

- If you already have ulcers or other digestive problems like chronic heartburn, stomach pain, nausea or diarrhea, stop drinking coffee for a couple of months, including decaf. See if it makes a difference for you.

■ Don't drink coffee on an empty stomach. Always protect the lining of the stomach from coffee's irritating effects by eating something along with it.

■ It's the roasting process that produces a lot of the irritating oils in coffee. So if and when you do drink coffee, stick to lighter roasts, which are less likely to irritate the digestive tract.

■ If you choose to drink decaffeinated coffee, select the water-processed kind, which doesn't have any added chemicals to increase digestive upset.

■ If you're taking an anti-ulcer drug, don't drink coffee, or you may be wasting an expensive medication.

Exercise

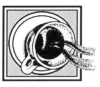

About exercise

Regular exercise has been advocated for many years in the United States because of its numerous health benefits. These benefits include lowering blood pressure, decreasing the incidence of heart attacks and vascular disease, maintaining muscle strength, increasing metabolism and relieving tension and depression.

The recent proliferation of gyms and health clubs attests to Americans' concern about their health. Average people now compete as amateurs in sports like cycling races, marathons and triathlons that were once popular only among athletes trained at a much higher fitness level. Amateurs and professionals alike are always seeking ways to improve their performance, either through new training methods or with dietary additions and changes.

What research has discovered

■ Caffeine is considered an *ergogenic* aid (a substance that increases one's ability to do physical work), as it can increase endurance and delay fatigue. It also increases restlessness.

Because of these effects, athletes have experimented with drinking coffee before athletic events—some have even used caffeine suppositories in an effort to improve their performance. As with other effects of caffeine, individuals vary in their response to its ergogenic properties.

▮ Caffeine stimulates the release of fats into the bloodstream. The body then uses these fats as fuel for muscular activity, rather than the glycogen it would normally use.

It's thought that caffeine helps athletes who exert for long periods of time delay their point of exhaustion, by saving their glycogen for later. It's not known yet whether this effect, like others, wears off with habitual coffee drinking (again, this may vary according to individual genetic differences).

This isn't such an advantage for more casual exercise, which isn't as likely to deplete glycogen stores; we have enough to supply energy for one and a half to two hours of exercise.

▮ One study found that well-trained competitive cyclists were able to pedal harder and endure 20% longer after drinking coffee. The study also found that drinking a couple of cups of coffee on the morning of a race improved runners' race times by as much as 16%.

- A small study of nine men found that caffeine didn't improve performance where maximum power or strength was required. Nor did they find that it helped with preventing short-term fatigue.

- Because caffeine increases alertness and improves reaction time, it can improve performance in sports like tennis, racquetball and ping pong, which rely on those qualities.

- Coffee is a *diuretic*, which means it increases the amount you urinate—by as much as 30%, for up to three hours, which can be quite inconvenient during competitive events!

This effect can also lead to more rapid dehydration in someone who is exercising long and hard, and thereby already losing a lot of fluids by sweating. Body minerals like sodium, potassium and calcium are also lost in sweating and urination, which can result in extreme fatigue.

- Other ill effects of coffee drinking, like heart palpitations and jitters, may inhibit athletic performance.

- Despite caffeine's mixed effects on athletic performance, the International

Olympic Committee disqualifies athletes if the concentration of caffeine in their urine is over a certain amount. Researchers have found that it takes more than eight cups of coffee drunk all at once to attain a disqualification level of caffeine, which would make it obvious that the athlete had deliberately taken a very large dose in order to artificially boost his or her performance.

What you can do

- Since coffee's effects vary among individuals, try a couple of cups of coffee before exercise or an athletic event and see if it seems to help you perform better. Keep in mind, though, that the effects of drinking more than two cups may hinder rather than help you.

- Be extremely careful about drinking coffee before exercising in hot weather; dehydration can be dangerous. It would be healthier to skip the coffee unless you take great care to replenish yourself with other fluids.

- If you experience irregular heartbeats or heart palpitations while exercising after drinking coffee, stop exercising immediately.

Fibrocystic breasts

About fibrocystic breast condition

Fibrocystic breast condition is caused by an increased growth of benign, fibrous tissue and cysts in the breasts. This process produces hard lumps which are often painful. The condition is linked to a higher risk of breast cancer.

The severity of fibrocystic breast condition tends to fluctuate, especially with the menstrual cycle, as the breasts are stimulated by higher estrogen levels. The breasts become noticeably lumpier and more tender a week or two before the menstrual period starts.

During this premenstrual time, there's also more blood flow and a greater accumulation of fluid in the breasts, which can aggravate a fibrocystic condition. Peak discomfort can range from mildly sensitive to very painful.

Fibrocystic breast condition is quite common, and often disappears by itself after menopause. Based on the number of women who seek medical care, it affects about 50% of women between the ages of 30 and 50. Based on autopsy reports, however, about 90% of American women have some degree of this condition.

This finding has led some theorists to wonder if fibrocystic breasts are a normal condition, which becomes abnormal and painful only when aggravated by outside factors.

What research has discovered

📭 The natural fluctuation in fibrocystic breast condition makes it difficult to study. Most research has found little evidence that drinking coffee actually causes the condition.

But one study of 1,700 women showed that those who drank four or more cups of coffee a day were twice as likely to have fibrocystic breasts as those who didn't drink coffee. And research into whether cutting out coffee drinking reduces or eliminates the lumps and pain have usually found that it does.

📭 Some of coffee's components have a mild estrogenlike effect on the body. Since estrogen is responsible for premenstrual tenderness in the breasts, this may be one reason coffee aggravates an existing fibrocystic condition.

What you can do

📭 If you're suffering from the discomfort of fibrocystic breasts, try removing coffee from your diet. (Switching to decaf won't necessarily help this problem, as decaf contains chemicals like theo-bromine and theophylline which are also considered aggravating factors.)

■ If you don't have fibrocystic breasts, but your breasts do get very tender right before your period, try eliminating or drastically cutting down on coffee just during the week or two before your period.

Headaches

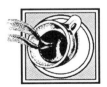

About headaches

Headaches are the most commonly-reported type of pain—severe headaches afflict millions of people each year. The pain doesn't actually originate in the brain, which has no sensory nerves, but in the membranes around the brain and in the scalp's muscles and blood vessels. It may be felt either all over the head or in just one place, and it may move around during a particular episode.

Tension in the head and neck muscles, brought on by emotional or physical stress, accounts for 90% of all headaches. Another 2%—*pathological* headaches—are caused by physical problems like head injury, infected sinuses, glaucoma, hemorrhage and tumors.

The remaining 8% are *vascular* headaches, which are caused by changes in the diameter of blood vessels (particularly dilation). Migraines are a type of vascular headache. Substances that dilate blood vessels, like alcohol, can cause vascular headaches. Substances that constrict blood vessels, like caffeine, help alleviate vascular headaches.

What research has discovered

- Caffeine is often added to pain medications because it improves their absorption and increases their *analgesic* (pain-killing) effect. Ergotamine tartrate, one of the most common drugs for migraines, usually has some effect if taken during the first hour of an attack. When caffeine is added, its effect is doubled (this ergotamine/caffeine combination goes by the trade names Cafergot and Wigraine).

  One study done on both animals and humans found that caffeine itself has analgesic properties comparable to Tylenol—although how it kills pain isn't known yet.

- The caffeine in a strong cup of coffee can help relieve a migraine, or even abort it, if consumed in the very early stage of a headache. But like other drugs, it probably won't help if the pain is already strongly throbbing or has been under way for an hour or more. (Unfortunately, caffeine can also delay sleep, which is one of the most therapeutic treatments for migraines.)

- Heavy coffee drinking can cause blood vessels to adapt to a semiconstricted state. Then, when caffeine levels in the blood decrease, the ensuing dilation of the blood vessels can trigger headaches. These are called "rebound" headaches because of the cycle of constriction and dilation, which can lead to a pattern of daily headaches.

■ Quitting coffee abruptly or changing drinking patterns can cause mild to severe vascular headaches. People who quit "cold turkey" almost always experience this. People whose consumption varies (between weekdays and weekends, for example) may also fall victim to withdrawal headaches.

What you can do

■ If you get migraines, try drinking a strong cup of coffee as soon as you feel one starting or about to start. Drinking more than that may prevent you from sleeping.

■ Drinking a cup or two of strong coffee may help decrease the discomfort of a hangover headache.

■ Limit your coffee intake to two cups a day in order to avoid rebound headaches.

■ Help prevent headaches by avoiding stress and other environmental and dietary triggers, and trying relaxation exercises, yoga, biofeedback or massage.

■ If you're getting headaches for no apparent reason and the suggestions given here don't help, call your doctor.

■ If you're quitting or cutting back on coffee, decrease your withdrawal headache pain by following the tips in the chapter on cutting back or quitting at the back of the book.

The heart

About the heart

Although many people survive heart attacks, disorders of the heart and blood vessels have been the leading cause of death in industrialized societies. Heart attacks can occur at any age, but most strike people 40 to 60 years old, particularly the obese and physically inactive. Due to increased public awareness of the importance of diet, weight control, exercise, stress reduction, regular physicals and early detection of problems, the incidence of heart disease is going down.

The normal resting rate of the heart is 60 to 100 beats per minute, depending on the age and physical condition of the individual. An abnormality in the heart's rhythm, called an *arrhythmia*, is experienced as fluttering or pounding of the heart, commonly known as "palpitations." They can be very scary experiences, but aren't usually dangerous.

Caffeine can cause arrhythmias and significantly speed up the rate of the heart. If you drink a lot of coffee but aren't used to it, your resting heart rate may accelerate as much as 10-20 beats per minute. In some people, caffeine can cause *tachycardia*, a rate of 100–160 beats per minute.

What research has discovered

▶ Research into the effects of coffee drinking on heart disease has produced very mixed results, greatly confusing the public. Each new study seems to contradict the one preceding it. Many studies haven't been able to confirm any link, while others have shown a substantially increased risk of heart attack among coffee drinkers.

For example, a Harvard study of 45,000 people found absolutely no increased risk of heart disease from drinking as much as six cups of regular coffee a day (although it did find a risk increase from drinking decaf). But this study included only men and all of them were health professionals. The results may have been skewed by the limited group it studied.

Another study done recently by Kaiser Permanente in Oakland, California, looked at 100,000 health plan members, of both sexes and from various racial, social and economic backgrounds. This study found that heavy coffee drinkers had a 40% greater risk of heart attack.

▶ Many studies have failed to account for other factors that could lead to heart disease, like smoking, a high-fat diet and a sedentary lifestyle. Some researchers have argued that these particular factors couldn't be eliminated from studies without eliminating the heavy coffee drinkers, since they frequently have all of these unhealthy habits.

One study of 129,000 people took into account the smoking habits and cholesterol levels of the participants. It found heart attacks to be slightly more common among heavy coffee drinkers.

But the researcher cautioned that something other than coffee—emotional stress, for instance—might be to blame. (Since people tend to drink more coffee when under a lot of stress, it may be the stress, not the coffee, that's causing the problem.)

The Harvard study mentioned above found a significantly increased risk of heart attack among decaf drinkers. Another study of 13,000 people found that decaf drinkers had the same increased risk as regular coffee drinkers. So chemicals other than caffeine may be responsible for the increased risk.

Tannin, which exists in coffee and black teas, has been found to damage the heart muscle in rats (animal studies like this usually use very high doses, though). Coffee's effect on cholesterol levels might also contribute to an increased risk of heart attack. No one knows yet for sure.

■ Even small amounts of caffeine can stimulate the heart muscle. It increases the force of contractions and affects the heart rate. A lot of caffeine can overstimulate the heart and cause scary and uncomfortable palpitations. But again, we all vary in our susceptibility. It appears that habitual coffee drinkers build up a tolerance to this effect of caffeine.

Heavy coffee drinkers are more likely to have arrhythmias called *premature ventricular contractions* (PVCs). These aren't particularly serious for healthy hearts, but for people who already have heart disease, PVCs have been linked with heart attacks.

■ One recent study found that six or more cups of coffee a day can exacerbate an existing arrhythmia. Studies using lower doses haven't always shown this to be true.

■ Caffeine activates *platelets*, a part of blood that promotes coagulation. Platelet activation is thought to be a factor leading to heart disease.

- Coffee drinking combined with another risk factor, like smoking, significantly increases your risk of heart disease.

What you can do

- If you have a family history of heart disease, are in any way predisposed to it, or already have some kind of heart irregularity, limit or cut out your coffee intake.

- If you don't have heart problems or a family history of heart disease, but occasionally or frequently experience palpitations from coffee drinking, just cutting back some on your intake may take care of the problem. Be aware, though, that as you get older this sensitivity may increase, and you may have to cut back even more.

- If you're recovering from a heart attack or heart surgery—a recuperative time during which heart rate and rhythm problems commonly occur—it's probably wise to stay away from coffee.

Infertility

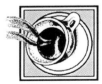

About infertility

In the last ten years, the problem of infertility has been on the rise in the United States. Almost three million American couples very much want to have a child, but can't. Approximately one out of every six couples will seek the help of an infertility specialist.

Infertility is usually defined as no pregnancy after a year of intercourse without using birth control. About 40% of the causes of infertility are found in the woman, 40% in the man and 20% in both people.

Conception and bringing the fetus to term depend on many complex processes in both the male and female bodies. Failure or interruption of any of these processes can hamper the egg from being fertilized by the sperm, implanted in the womb and developing normally.

What research has discovered

■ Recent research suggests that coffee may affect women's fertility. A study by the National Institute of Environmental Health Sciences revealed that women who drank more than one cup of coffee a day reduced their likelihood of conceiving by one-half. The researchers haven't yet identified how coffee interferes with the fertilization process.

This study—the first to find a link between coffee and impaired fertility—didn't measure the influence of other factors like age, nutrition, exercise, stress or differences in drinking water. A subsequent study, published in 1990, suggested that people's caffeine intake is associated with their age, weight, and use of alcohol and tobacco. Theoretically, all these factors can affect fertility, so they may be the culprits, not caffeine.

■ Caffeine from the woman's bloodstream can penetrate the *blastocyst*, or fertilized egg, right before it embeds in the lining of the womb. This may hinder the blastocyst from implanting, and if it doesn't implant, it'll be swept out with the next menstrual period.

■ Research has also looked at caffeine's effects on sperm. If a very high concentration of caffeine is added directly to semen just prior to artificial insemination, sperm mobility increases. Apparently, a woman's twice as likely to get pregnant under these circumstances. It's unknown whether there are any negative side effects of this procedure.

Drinking two to three cups of coffee a day has been shown to increase sperm mobility. This may, in turn, enhance fertility, but it also increases the incidence of abnormally formed sperm. The abnormal ones compete just as well as normal sperm to get inside the egg, but abnormal sperm may contribute to miscarriage.

Having five, six or more cups of coffee daily appears to make sperm sluggish. Drinking four or more cups a day combined with smoking over 20 cigarettes a day has been shown to decrease sperm mobility and increase the percentage of dead sperm in semen.

- Caffeine isn't stored in the body, so it won't have a permanent effect on your fertility. The coffee you drank last month won't affect you this month.

What you can do

- If you're a woman and are having difficulty getting pregnant, switch to decaf or cut down to no more than one cup of caffeinated coffee a day. If you've been trying to get pregnant for a long time, you may want to eliminate coffee and other sources of caffeine altogether.

- If you're the male half of an infertile couple, drinking a couple of cups of coffee a day may help you, but it also may deform your sperm. Drinking more than that may hinder your fertility, especially if you're also a heavy smoker.

- What you *can't* do is keep yourself from getting pregnant by drinking a lot of coffee. If you don't want to get pregnant, coffee may diminish your fertility, but don't forget, we all differ genetically in how we metabolize and respond to caffeine. So don't even think of substituting coffee for your regular method of birth control.

Mental alertness

About mental alertness

One's state of mental alertness, capacity for mental work and overall energy level generally depend on a number of factors, including physical and emotional well-being, adequate sleep and good nutrition.

The desire to increase mental alertness and vitality is one of the main reasons people drink coffee. The caffeine in coffee stimulates the central nervous system, which is made up of the brain and spinal cord. It directly stimulates brain cells—especially in the cerebral cortex, the most highly evolved part of the brain, which is involved in all intellectual functions. This stimulation also affects moods and emotions.

What research has discovered

☛ Drinking one or two cups of coffee can reduce fatigue and drowsiness—at least temporarily. Drinking more than that will change a person's brain activity from that of an awake but resting person to that of an alert and active person (as indicated by increased beta brain waves).

■ Some experts believe caffeine helps us think more clearly and improves mental efficiency and alertness. One study found that caffeine can improve reading speed without causing an increase in errors. Another found that even a small dose of caffeine (32 mg.—equivalent to about a third of a cup of coffee) on an empty stomach improved reaction time, concentration, and accuracy on mental performance tests.

■ Apparently we don't build up a tolerance to caffeine's effect on alertness. Moderate and heavy coffee drinkers in the above study showed the same improvement in performance as those who didn't normally drink coffee at all.

■ Although drinking a small amount of coffee can improve work efficiency, drinking more than one or two cups may be detrimental. After several cups of coffee, many people become nervous and restless, which can affect concentration.

■ Coffee drinking has been shown to improve performance in such tasks as driving, perhaps because it shortens reaction time. But it actually hinders performance in activities that require fine motor coordination, probably because of the nervousness, hand tremors and muscle tension it causes.

■ Many people think that coffee can sober you up quickly after a few alcoholic drinks. Wrong! Although it may make a drunk feel and act more alert, no amount of coffee can shorten the time the body needs to break down and eliminate alcohol. It takes about an hour to metabolize the alcohol in one hard drink, glass of wine or can of beer.

In fact, the combination of caffeine and alcohol can be particularly dangerous: when intoxicated people feel more alert, they may think they can do things they're still not capable of, like driving safely.

Caffeine acts as a mood elevator and can make people feel more "up" for a couple of hours. The molecular structure of caffeine is very similar to a brain chemical that can make you feel "down," and it fools brain cells into binding with it instead of the natural chemical, thus preventing its depressant function. So it not only stimulates you, it also blocks the neurotransmitter that makes you feel "down."

But when this effect wears off, you may feel even worse than before you drank the coffee. This coffee hangover, consisting of depression, fatigue and sometimes headache, is a common after-effect of stimulants. The ensuing need to regain a sense of well-being causes a craving for more coffee, creating a cycle that can lead to psychological as well as physical dependence.

What you can do

■ If you want to use coffee to improve mental performance, drink just one cup in the morning and another late in the afternoon. That's enough to give you the mental performance boost that you want at the times you probably need it most, while avoiding the detrimental effects of too much coffee. Drink decaffeinated coffee or some other beverage in between those two cups.

■ If you're driving and feeling sleepy, drinking a couple of cups of coffee should help you stay alert.

■ Don't expect coffee to make up for a night of drinking alcohol—it won't make it safe for you to drive yourself home.

■ Don't use coffee as an anti-depressant; you're only creating a vicious cycle of physical and psychological dependence. Find other ways to make yourself feel good, like going for a walk in the fresh air and sunlight or calling a friend.

■ Get adequate rest. A series of late nights in a row will definitely decrease your alertness and energy. Using coffee to keep yourself going in a situation like that is like kicking a dead-tired horse.

■ Get regular exercise to help shake off drowsiness, increase your energy and alertness and put yourself in a better mood. Exercising is much healthier than depending on coffee for these benefits.

PMS

About premenstrual syndrome

Premenstrual syndrome (PMS) is estimated to affect 50% or more of American women. This syndrome comprises over a hundred uncomfortable symptoms and usually starts one or two weeks before a woman's menstrual period.

An individual woman affected by PMS often experiences as many as ten to twelve of these symptoms, at various levels of severity. Symptoms include fluid retention, bloating, weight gain, sugar craving, headaches, irritability, breast tenderness, fatigue, depression, changes in sleep patterns, oily hair and skin breakouts.

The symptoms can get progressively worse until the period starts, and sometimes last two or three days into the period. This means that millions of women spend one or two weeks out of every month feeling awful. Because PMS usually gets worse as women age (until menopause, of course), those women who are in their thirties and forties often experience it more severely than their younger counterparts.

Only in recent years has the syndrome been officially acknowledged and named. Previously, doctors would explain the symptoms away as psychological, stress-related or even imaginary.

63

Fortunately, the new awareness has led to a lot of research into related areas, including the effect of dietary substances like caffeine on the incidence and severity of PMS.

What research has discovered

■ There's definitely more than one cause of PMS, but several studies have linked caffeine consumption to a higher incidence of symptoms. Among those that seem to be exacerbated by caffeine are tension, irritability, anxiety, fatigue, sleep disturbance and breast tenderness.

■ One of the more recent studies on the link between caffeine and PMS was done on female tea drinkers in China. This study was carried out by an epidemiologist who had previously done studies in the United States on the effects of coffee, tea and cola on PMS sufferers (all these beverages showed strong links to PMS).

She found the Chinese women to be an ideal group to study because their lifestyle didn't include other PMS factors like lack of exercise or a diet high in fat or sugar. The majority of the women rode their bikes daily as a mode of transportation, and didn't use alcohol, tobacco or oral contraceptives; and their only source of caffeine was tea.

The researcher found a very high correlation between PMS symptoms and tea consumption: the heavier the consumption, the higher the incidence of symptoms. The women who drank four and a half or more cups a day were almost ten times more likely to have PMS symptoms as those who drank none.

Since coffee has more caffeine than the green tea drunk in China, one could expect coffee drinkers to be even more likely to suffer the discomforts of PMS. (And since the results of all studies linking caffeinated drinks to PMS have been similar, it's unlikely that anything besides caffeine was responsible for this study's results.)

☛ Some of coffee's components have a mild estrogen-like effect on the body. Since estrogen is responsible for many PMS symptoms, this may be another way in which coffee aggravates premenstrual syndrome.

What you can do

☛ If you suffer from PMS, try eliminating coffee and other sources of caffeine from your diet. Stay away from caffeine at least a few months to see if it makes a difference in how you feel.

☛ If you suffer from PMS but can't face giving up coffee, try cutting way back or eliminating it during the week or two before your period starts (doctors often recommend cutting out all factors that could affect PMS during the second half of the menstrual cycle). That may be enough to reduce PMS symptoms and improve you feel.

Pregnancy

About pregnancy

During pregnancy the mother's body acts as an incubator for the fetus. Oxygen and nutrients pass from the mother's blood through the placenta into the blood of the fetus.

It was formerly thought that the placenta acted as a barrier to toxins, allowing only beneficial nutrients to reach the baby. But it's now known that most chemical substances flow directly across the placenta from the mother's bloodstream to the baby's bloodstream. Any drug that crosses the placenta is potentially hazardous to the fetus, especially during the first three months, when the brain, face, organs and limbs are forming.

A quantity of drug or chemical that's safe for the mother may be harmful to the fetus. That's why health-care providers strongly advise pregnant women not to take any drugs that they really don't need.

What research has discovered

■ Animal studies have linked high blood levels of caffeine to premature birth, delivery complications, low birth weight and birth defects. (Keep in mind, though, that these studies were all done using very, very high doses of caffeine.)

- Studies of coffee's effects on human pregnancy have found an increase in the rate of miscarriages, stillbirths and low-birth-weight babies among coffee-drinking mothers. Not all studies on humans have been able to confirm these findings, however.

  Low birth weight (usually defined as a newborn weight of less than five and a half pounds) has a significant impact on the well-being of the newborn. These babies tend to have greater susceptibility to illness, greater nutritional needs, decreased ability to maintain normal body temperature and an increased risk of death. They also have a harder time enduring the stress of labor and birth.

- The clearest evidence from human studies indicates that drinking more than one cup of coffee a day during pregnancy can slow fetal growth and cause low birth weight. One study, very carefully designed to eliminate other factors, showed that two to three cups of coffee a day doubled the risk of a low-birthweight infant. More than three cups a day quadrupled the risk.

- Pregnant women are slower to metabolize caffeine and clear it out of the body—about three times slower than nonpregnant women. This slower clearing rate is especially true in the third trimester, normally the time of greatest weight gain for the fetus. The effects of a couple of cups of coffee can be quite prolonged, lasting days, and the amount of caffeine circulating in the bloodstream can rise above what a nonpregnant coffee drinker would experience. This extended high level of caffeine is passed on to the fetus.

- As mentioned in the chapter on breast-feeding, fetuses and newborns haven't developed the enzymes necessary to metabolize caffeine. Instead, they must eliminate it through their urine, a much slower process than cleansing through the liver, as more mature bodies do. So caffeine stays in their systems much longer, and can accumulate to toxic levels.

- A study done on women 32 to 36 weeks pregnant showed that when they drank two cups of coffee in the morning, the fetuses' breathing rates doubled and their heart rates fell significantly. Two cups of decaffeinated coffee also stimulated fetal breathing activity and caused fetal heart rate to fall, although to a lesser degree. These symptoms are associated with the fetus being under stress.

- Breech births are more common in women who drink more than five cups of coffee a day. In a breech birth, the baby's bottom emerges first, rather than the head. These births involve more potential complications for the baby during labor and delivery, some life-threatening.

■ Caffeine is a *mutagen*—a substance with the potential to damage genes. It's very similar in structure to DNA, which forms our genetic makeup. It's thought that caffeine has the potential to interfere with DNA duplication by substituting for some of its components, possibly causing genetic defects.

■ Some very recent research has shown that diabetes is most common in countries where there's heavy coffee consumption. One theoretical explanation is that since caffeine from the mother's blood can reach the fetus, it may build up in the fetus' pancreas and damage the cells that would later produce insulin.

What you can do

■ During the first three formative months of pregnancy, when the fetus is extremely susceptible to developmental harm, you should completely eliminate coffee.

■ During the remainder of your pregnancy, drink no more than one cup a day or switch to decaf. To play it really safe, cut out coffee altogether.

Sleep
disturbance

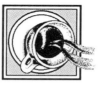

About sleep

Most people spend about a third of their lives sleeping. No matter how active or sedentary their lifestyles, they nearly all need some amount of sleep every 24 hours in order to function well and feel rested.

But there's a huge difference in the amount of sleep people need—some get along quite well on three hours a night, whereas others must have ten. The average adult needs seven to eight hours daily.

Whatever the length of your typical night's sleep, there are several stages to it, all of which are important for your mental and physical well-being. The *NREM (non-rapid-eye-movement)* part, which makes up 80% of the sleep cycle, comprises four stages of progressively deeper sleep. The *REM (rapid-eye-movement)* part, during which dreaming occurs, makes up the remainder of the cycle.

If any of these stages is disturbed, the body tries to catch up on subsequent nights. This "sleep debt" can lead to a decreased ability to concentrate and perform tasks during the day. Extreme sleep deprivation can cause paranoia and hallucinations.

One out of every three American adults regularly experiences sleep disturbance (problems either falling asleep or staying asleep). There are now over 200 sleep disorder clinics in the US. Sleeping medications are widely prescribed, although many of them result in physical and psychological dependence.

What research has discovered

▣ Caffeine decreases the quality of sleep and has been found to be one of the leading causes of sleep disturbance.

▣ A Japanese study showed that it can take four times longer than normal to get to sleep after drinking a strong cup of coffee (containing about 150 mg. of caffeine).

▣ Drinking one or two cups of coffee before bed substantially reduces sleep time. One study of people over 50 found their sleep was reduced by as much as two hours. Since people in this age group sleep less anyway, this represents a proportionally greater loss than for younger people.

▣ When compared to abstainers, heavy coffee drinkers toss and turn more in bed, delaying the onset of sleep. This may be because caffeine increases muscle tension and restlessness. Frequent movements also cause frequent waking.

- Caffeine consumption before bedtime causes people to be awakened more easily by sudden noises.

- Brain wave studies show that caffeine disturbs sleep most during the first three to four hours. It shortens the deep sleep and increases the light sleep parts of NREM stages (whether or not caffeine affects the REM phase of sleep is still unknown).

- Coffee drinkers have been found to be sleepier and groggier than non-coffee drinkers when they get up in the morning, causing them to depend on coffee to get them going. Such grogginess may be the result of their entering caffeine withdrawal during the night. It may also be that drinking coffee kept them from sleeping well in the first place—or that both of these factors disturbed their sleep.

- One researcher has theorized that people who only drink coffee early in the day may actually sleep better because by evening they are experiencing the grogginess and fatigue of caffeine withdrawal.

- People differ in their susceptibility to caffeine's effects on sleep. Some people claim they can go right to sleep even after drinking more than one cup of strong coffee, and experience no disturbance at all. But they're the exceptions—caffeine's disruption of sleep is one of its most commonly observed and discussed problems.

■ Caffeine can decrease the effect of sleep medications, creating a temptation to take more of them.

What you can do

■ If coffee disturbs your sleep, don't drink it later than four or five hours before bedtime. Other options are to eliminate coffee, switch to decaf or only drink it early in the day.

Some people need more than a day to clear caffeine from their bodies. For them, even drinking coffee early in the day may disturb their sleep. Generally, the closer to bedtime you drink caffeinated coffee, the stronger the effect it will have.

■ If you don't want to give up your coffee, or even switch to decaf, try countering its effects by having warm milk or a calcium/magnesium drink like *Calm*, before going to bed.

Some stretching and deep breathing at bedtime may also help relieve some of the muscle tension and restlessness that caffeine causes and enable you to get to sleep more easily. A warm bath or shower might also help.

- If you drink a lot of coffee one evening and it affects your sleep, make everything optimal for sleeping well the next night (avoid coffee, in particular). You'll need to repay your sleep debt.

- If you're taking sleeping pills, it may be coffee drinking that caused you to need them in the first place. If you eliminate coffee or switch to decaf, you may eventually find that you don't need the pills anymore. But don't quit taking them abruptly, as you can experience withdrawal symptoms. Check with your doctor to find out how to gradually reduce the amount you take.

- Doctors should ask their patients about their coffee drinking habits before prescribing sleeping pills for them. Likewise, you should inform your doctor of your coffee-drinking habits before getting a prescription.

Tobacco withdrawal

About tobacco withdrawal

Only recently has smoking been recognized as a major health hazard. It's estimated that cigarette smoking is responsible for at least one out of every seven deaths in the United States. It contributes to heart disease, lung disease, lung cancer and other cancers, as well as many other physical maladies. Smokers are now frequently advised by their physicians to quit as soon as possible (whether or not they're showing symptoms of its harmful effects).

The overall proportion of the population that smokes has gone down substantially in the last 30 years. The proportion of women who smoke has increased, however: there are now almost as many female smokers as male smokers. In the past, smoking-related deaths among men have far outnumbered those among women. But health-care providers have already seen an increase in smoking-related diseases among women.

Cigarettes are so addictive that smokers usually have an extremely difficult time quitting. Most need some kind of help to persevere against withdrawal symptoms like extreme nervousness and craving. Fortunately, there are plenty of aids to choose from: behavior modification, hypnosis, acupuncture, nicotine chewing gum and many others.

In spite of all the help available, the success rate for quitting is low. In fact, many smokers can tell you they've "quit" a few times already.

What research has discovered

■ Caffeine remains in smokers' blood only about half as long as in non-smokers' blood. This is because the tar in cigarettes increases the rate at which liver enzymes metabolize caffeine.

As a result, smokers have to drink a lot more coffee than non-smokers to get the same effect from it (research has found that smokers do tend to drink more coffee than non-smokers). This can cause big problems for people who are trying to quit smoking.

The rate of caffeine metabolism goes down within a few days of smoking the last cigarette, but an ex-smoker will usually continue to drink as much coffee as before quitting. This leads to very high caffeine levels in the blood. In one study of participants in a stop-smoking program, measurements at 12 and 26 weeks showed a caffeine concentration level in their blood that was 250% higher than before they began the program.

- Tobacco withdrawal symptoms include irritability, nervousness, anxiety attacks and sleep disturbance—the very conditions that a high blood level of caffeine will cause! So the person who has just quit smoking and continues to drink as much coffee as before has the distinct likelihood of becoming a nervous wreck.

- Smokers usually depend on cigarettes to calm them down (the nicotine they contain acts as a tranquilizer). Because smokers associate smoking with relaxing, the condition of intense nervousness caused by the combination of withdrawal and a high blood level of caffeine makes it all the more likely they'll start smoking again.

What you can do

- If you intend to quit smoking, help yourself along by either cutting out coffee, cutting back or switching to decaf. Changing your habits will reduce your need for nicotine's tranquilizing effect, and it's especially important if:

—you're predisposed to heart disease, since the higher caffeine levels in your blood will increase your risk for heart problems

—you're pregnant, since your baby would be getting a higher dose of caffeine along with you.

Vision problems

About vision problems

The eye is very complex, and good vision depends on the optimal health and functioning of many structures within it. The elasticity of the lens, health of the optic nerves and quality of the circulation in the eye all affect its normal functions.

Blood and fluid called *aqueous humor* normally flow through our eyes, nourishing them and maintaining an *intraocular* pressure (pressure within the eye) which stabilizes everything they contain. If the aqueous humor fails to drain normally, the increased intraocular pressure can damage the optic nerves and may lead to blindness. That's the end result of glaucoma (if untreated), a disease that's a major cause of blindness in the United States.

Glaucoma is more common in older people, black people, diabetics and those with a family history of glaucoma. It's been estimated that a million Americans have this disease and don't even know it. Early diagnosis and treatment are extremely important in preventing vision loss due to glaucoma.

What research has discovered

▶ The caffeine in coffee causes small blood vessels in the eyes to constrict. This constriction reduces the blood vessels' ability to provide nutrients to the eyes and to remove waste products. It also contributes to intraocular pressure.

▶ One study on glaucoma patients found that drinking two cups of coffee caused a sustained increase in intraocular pressure. In people who didn't have glaucoma, it took twice as much coffee to produce the same increase.

Not all researchers have found a significant change in pressure in either group from drinking two cups of coffee. Some authorities feel that this discrepancy is probably due to individual differences in susceptibility to the effects of caffeine.

▶ Drinking four or more cups of coffee a day significantly increases the intraocular pressure in most people's eyes. Researchers think that coffee drinking alone isn't enough to cause glaucoma, but that if you have a family history of glaucoma, it could definitely increase your risk.

▶ The highest increase in intraocular pressure was found in people who rapidly gulped down their coffee, consuming four cups in one hour. People who consumed the same amount more slowly had less of an increase in pressure.

- Eye tests show that coffee adversely affects the eyes' ability to do close work, like reading, by limiting the ability of the eyes to focus at close range.

- A group of students was given special glasses, known to improve reading ability, to see if the students would improve their reading scores with this aid. It was found that the students who drank six or fewer cups of coffee a week did improve their scores with the glasses. The students who drank 21 to 42 cups of coffee a week showed no improvement.

What you can do

- If you have glaucoma, a family history of glaucoma or are otherwise at risk for developing the disease, drink only decaf or quit altogether. This also applies if you already have vision problems and wear glasses or contact lenses.

- If you need to do a lot of reading or other close work, avoid drinking a lot of caffeinated coffee. A small amount may help you with reading though (see the chapter on mental alertness).

- Hot tip for contact lens wearers: because coffee acts as a diuretic, drinking a lot of it can make your eyes so dry that wearing contacts becomes very uncomfortable. If you're having this kind of problem, see if it helps to cut back on or eliminate coffee.

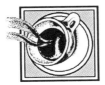

Vitamin and mineral loss

About vitamins and minerals

Vitamins and minerals are essential to a healthful diet, and since our bodies generally can't manufacture them, we depend on getting them from our food.

A nutritional deficiency can be caused by a poor diet or by toxic elements in it. A vitamin deficiency can affect the metabolism, brain, nerves, muscles, skin and bones. A mineral deficiency can affect cell metabolism, bones, teeth and the fluid balance in the body. Each vitamin or mineral generally plays a role in many bodily functions.

So well-being depends on maintaining a balance of these nutrients that enable all the biochemical reactions necessary for normal bodily functions.

What research has discovered

■ Coffee can't be considered a food because it doesn't aid in the repair or maintenance of tissues. Nor is it essential for any of the body's various physiological functions.

Coffee does contain sodium, magnesium, potassium and calcium, as well as lesser amounts of other minerals and trace elements. But it provides them in very small quantities when compared to those found in other mineral sources in our diets. And the caffeine in coffee actually inhibits the body's ability to absorb these nutrients.

Coffee *can* provide a significant source of niacin, but only people on severely deficient, near starvation diets would need such a supplement. (The uncomfortable symptoms of *pellagra*, the condition caused by extreme niacin deficiency, can be resolved by drinking coffee—although pellagra is hardly a common problem in the US and other industrialized nations.)

■ Research has shown that drinking three cups of coffee a day can cause a significant loss of calcium because caffeine inhibits the body's ability to absorb it.

We need calcium to keep our bones strong and to maintain healthy teeth. Studies on adult women have shown that heavy coffee drinking can lead to a loss of bone density, which can increase the risk of osteoporosis and broken bones.

■ Caffeinated coffee acts as a diuretic, increasing the amount you urinate by about 30% for up to three hours. This means further loss of calcium, potassium, magnesium and sodium, as these minerals are excreted in urine. (It can also cause you to be chronically dehydrated, particularly if your fluid intake consists only or mainly of coffee.)

Increased urination also drains the body of water-soluble vitamins (B and C). Water-soluble vitamins are extremely important for the body's normal functions, like digesting fats, carbohydrates and proteins, and maintaining a healthy heart, nerves, skin, muscles and bones (to name a few from a long list). They can't be stored in the body like the fat-soluble ones (A, D, E, and K), so deficiencies are more common. We need a fresh supply of vitamins B and C every day.

▪ Coffee drinking also causes iron loss because tannin—found in coffee and black tea—binds with iron and prevents its absorption into the bloodstream. One study showed that drinking one cup of coffee decreased the iron absorbed from a hamburger meal by a whopping 39%.

A study of pregnant women produced significant evidence that coffee drinking during pregnancy leads to *anemia* (deficiency in the blood's oxygen-carrying capacity) in the mother and child. The researchers theorized that this anemia resulted from the iron deficiency caused by coffee drinking.

▪ Coffee consumption can also cause loss of zinc, a mineral that affects our eyesight, immune system and sex drive, among many other functions.

What you can do

- If you're pregnant, or anemic (as is often the case with menstruating women), don't drink coffee. Decaf isn't safe either, since it also contains the tannins that lead to iron deficiency.

- Don't drink coffee at the same time you eat iron-rich foods like red meat, green leafy vegetables, iron fortified cereals or prune juice. Don't use it to wash down iron supplements or other vitamin or mineral supplements, either. You'd be wasting the supplements.

- If you're a woman of menopausal age, keep your coffee intake to a minimum or drink only decaf. Estrogen helps maintain bone mass, and after menopause, your ovaries no longer produce it. You're then at a higher risk for loss of bone density, which is called *osteoporosis*. Your bones need the calcium that you'd lose by drinking coffee.

- If you absolutely can't give up your coffee, take vitamin and mineral supplements each day (consult a nutrition specialist on what to take and how much). Have your supplements with water, juice or milk at some point during the day when you're not drinking coffee.

Weight loss

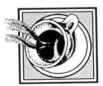

About weight loss

Americans are among the most overweight people in the world. We simply eat too much, and our diets consist of a lot of refined carbohydrates, sugar and fatty foods.

Furthermore, many Americans lead very sedentary lives. We're more dependent on the automobile than any other people in the world. The most exercise many Americans get is in walking to and from their cars.

Seriously overweight people are more at risk for developing a whole slew of illnesses, including diabetes, high blood pressure, heart disease, cancer and arthritis. So health care providers recommend maintaining normal weight to help ensure future good health.

Sometimes it seems like almost everyone in America is on a diet. But since many people are willing to risk their health on dangerous diets, it's apparently their appearance they're trying to improve.

The weight-reduction business is a multi-million dollar industry in the US. Fad diets come and go continually. Diet books become best-sellers.

Everyone's looking for a quick and easy way to lose weight.

Unfortunately, weight lost this way is usually gained back, since it's often water that was lost, not fat. Weight-loss experts have found that eating habits and lifestyles must change for successful, permanent weight loss to occur.

What research has discovered

- One of the few health benefits of coffee drinking is that it may help you to control your weight. The caffeine in one cup of brewed coffee can raise the rate at which you burn calories by 3–4% by speeding up your metabolism.

- In one study, participants took the caffeine equivalent of one cup of coffee every two hours for twelve hours. Their metabolic rates went up 5% and they burned an extra 110 calories a day. Other studies have shown metabolic increases of anywhere from 10% to 30%, depending on the amount of caffeine consumed, lasting three to four hours.

- Drinking caffeinated coffee with a meal increases the rate at which the food you consume will be converted into calorie-burning energy. This may be due to the increase in hydrochloric acid production in the stomach that coffee causes.

- If taken between meals, caffeinated coffee promotes fat burning by freeing fatty acids into the bloodstream. If taken on an empty stomach just before exercise, it enables the body to use fat rather than carbohydrates as fuel. Burning carbohydrates tends to increase the appetite, creating a vicious cycle for the overweight person.

A study focusing on obese people found that three eight-ounce cups of coffee a day helped their bodies burn more fat during exercise. Normally obese people tend to burn carbohydrates almost exclusively, rather than fat.

- The caffeine in coffee raises the body temperature, and calories must be burned in order to accomplish this.

- Caffeine initially suppresses the appetite, but it also stimulates the pancreas to release insulin, which eventually causes a drop in blood sugar, producing hunger and a let-down feeling.

What you can do

- You have to weigh all the possible adverse health effects of coffee drinking before using it as a weight loss aid. You'd have to drink six cups of coffee a day for slightly over a month just to lose one pound.

There's also some question as to whether habitual coffee drinkers continue to enjoy these benefits after developing a tolerance to caffeine. Lastly, using coffee in this way would be like using any other weight loss drug. It's not addressing the real issue: overeating and lack of exercise.

- If you're obese (20% or more over normal weight), drinking one or two cups of coffee before exercising should help you burn more fat rather than the carbohydrates that you would burn otherwise.

- If you're going to drink coffee at meal times in order to lose weight, have it after your meal rather than before or during it. This will protect your stomach lining from irritation by the coffee.

- Coffee is more likely to cause stomach pains and jittery nerves when drunk on an empty stomach. If you want to try drinking it before exercise and on an empty stomach, start with small amounts.

- When you experience the aftermath of hunger and letdown from coffee drinking, eat a low-calorie snack with natural sugars, like a piece of fruit, to pick you up again. You'll have to prepare yourself psychologically for this so that you don't binge on high-calorie sweets.

- Of course, if you're using coffee for weight loss, adding sugar or cream would be self-defeating.

Decaffeinated coffee

About decaffeinated coffee

Many of coffee's ill effects have been attributed to caffeine, which has prompted some coffee drinkers to switch to decaffeinated coffee in recent years. Decaffeination removes 97-98% of the caffeine from coffee beans.

But as you can see from previous chapters, it's not just caffeine that affects your health. The oils, acids, tannins and hundreds of other chemicals in both regular and decaffeinated coffee also cause physiological changes. Let's take a closer look at decaf to see whether it's really better for you.

Coffee beans are decaffeinated before they're roasted to avoid losing the flavors and aromas that roasting achieves. There are two main methods of decaffeination—by solvent and by water.

Benzene and trichloroethylene were two of the early solvents used to remove caffeine from coffee (trichlorethylene eventually replaced benzene completely because it was cheaper and less toxic). But as discussed in the chapter on cancer, trichloroethylene has shown evidence of causing pancreatic cancer. So it hasn't been used to decaffeinate coffee since the late seventies, when the FDA began investigating it as a possible carcinogen.

The solvent most often used now, methylene chloride, is supposedly safer but has a similar chemical structure to trichlorethylene. It's also toxic and can cause irregular or abnormal heartbeats, nausea and vomiting.

The methylene chloride is washed off the beans after the decaffeinating process, but a small amount remains; it's impossible to remove it all. The maximum residue allowed by the FDA is ten parts per million, or .00016 of an ounce per pound of coffee. The FDA considers this a safe level of exposure.

Some companies use another solvent, ethyl acetate. Ethyl acetate is found in common fruits like apples and bananas and is, therefore, considered safe for human consumption (it's approved by the FDA). Only very few companies use this rather than methyl chloride, though, because it's more expensive.

In the water-process method, coffee beans are soaked in water to remove the caffeine. This takes about eight hours, and a lot of soluble coffee solids are also absorbed into the water. Methylene chloride is then used to extract the caffeine from the liquid. Next, the solvent is stripped from the fluid which, in turn, is restored to the beans.

The water process is also called the indirect method of decaffeination since the solvent never comes in direct contact with the beans, and the chemical can (supposedly) be entirely removed from the fluid before it's returned to the beans. Another advantage of the water process is that it removes slightly more caffeine than the solvent method—98% rather than 97%.

A company in Switzerland has developed a process whereby a natural absorbent like sucrose, glucose and/or another hydrocarbon, rather than artificial solvents, is used to remove the caffeine from the water. This decaffeinated coffee is sold as Swiss water-processed decaf.

Water-processed decaf is more expensive than coffee decaffeinated with methyl chloride, and the Swiss-processed beans tend to be even a bit more expensive. As the demand for it increases, so should the supply, and prices will come down.

What you can do

☞ To play it safe, use only water-processed decaffeinated coffee, which hasn't come in direct contact with the solvent. The best is Swiss water-processed coffee since it uses the safest substance(s) to extract caffeine.

☞ If you have ulcers or digestive problems of any kind, switching to decaf isn't the solution, since decaf still contains the acids and oils that cause digestive problems (see the chapter on digestive disorders). You're better off not drinking coffee.

☞ If you have high cholesterol, decaf isn't really a viable alternative to regular coffee, since the chemical in coffee that affects cholesterol—although still not identified—doesn't appear to be caffeine (see the chapter on cholesterol).

Cutting back or quitting

About cutting back or quitting

If you've decided to make some changes in your coffee drinking habits, this chapter provides you with some tips for quitting, cutting back or switching to decaffeinated coffee. Changing habits is definitely not easy, but planning ahead can make all the difference, especially if you prepare yourself for success rather than failure.

Quitting coffee "cold turkey"—stopping your coffee intake all at once—can cause mild to severe headaches as well as other unpleasant side effects like nausea, anxiety, fatigue and depression. These are all signs that you've actually been addicted to coffee.

The withdrawal symptoms can last for several days, and it can take a few weeks to get back to feeling normal again. If you've been a heavy coffee drinker and quit cold turkey, you may also find it hard to concentrate at work for a few days. The methods suggested below will help minimize your discomfort.

Eventually you'll feel more awake and have a more even energy level throughout the day than when you were drinking coffee. A few weeks or months after quitting, most people come to realize that they feel much better without coffee—but you should be aware that it may take that long.

What you can do

📍 If you want to wean yourself off regular coffee by switching to decaf, start by substituting decaffeinated coffee for every other cup you drink or drink a half decaf/half regular brew. But be sure you don't start drinking more cups of coffee each day in order to get your usual dose of caffeine.

Keep to your usual number of cups and gradually increase the amount of decaf until it reaches 100%. Be especially careful in restaurants as waiters will often mistakenly give you regular coffee for refills even though you started with decaf.

📍 Some people dilute their coffee more and more with water until they're eventually just drinking hot water and then stick with hot water as a beverage.

📍 Another method is to cut back by one cup every three to four days until you're down to the amount you want to stay at (one or two cups a day) or until you have eliminated coffee altogether.

📍 If you're going to quit, choose a time when you're not going to be under a lot of stress (while relaxing on vacation would be a good time). Don't pick a period of year that's stressful socially or professionally (for example, avoid the holidays, or tax season, if you're an accountant).

- Exercise can be helpful when getting off coffee. Whatever form you choose—a short run or walk, yoga or stretching—can help energize you first thing in the morning instead of a cup of coffee. (Of course, exercise will also help release tension and relieve anxiety no matter when you do it.)

- Taking stress vitamins (especially B complex and C) and calcium and magnesium supplements can help calm your nerves when quitting. Check with a nutritional consultant for advice on appropriate doses.

- Line up a companion to back you up in your efforts. This could be a friend who has cut back or quit drinking coffee or someone who will be especially supportive of you during this time—someone who cares about you and your good health.

If and when you feel your resolve weakening, give that person a call. You could also arrange to have a couple of others give you a call each day over a two- to three-week period just to see how you're doing.

- If you live with other coffee drinkers, it'll help if they make the switch with you. After all, it's likely to improve their health and well-being too. It's a lot easier if everyone in a household makes the same dietary or lifestyle changes at the same time because it provides more support and less temptation.

- Plan ahead for this time. Look for coffee substitutes that you'd enjoy drinking. There are now many wonderful and delicious herbal teas easily available. You can also choose from a number of grain-based coffee substitutes like Cafix, Pero and Postum (my editor says "ick" as do a lot of people, but give them a try). Or try cold drinks like flavored mineral waters.

  If you still want some caffeine, try black tea. It'll provide you with a lower dose, without all the oils, acids and other chemicals that coffee contains. If you're used to having milk in your coffee, try drinking English Breakfast tea with milk in it, the way most English do—it has a taste appeal all its own.

- Provide lots of TLC for yourself. Get a massage. Take hot, soothing baths. Spend some relaxing time in nature. If you've used coffee drinking as a relaxation ritual in the past, it's especially important to find some substitutes.

■ Think of other things that will get you going in the morning instead of coffee. Exercise, again, would help. Rubbing down in the shower with a body brush or loofah sponge is also stimulating and will soon wake you up.

Good luck changing your coffee-drinking habits, if that's what you decide to do. I've quit drinking coffee twice and feel that I'm off it for keeps now. The first time I quit for two years and definitely felt better without it. But then I went through a stressful period and started drinking caffé lattes and strong coffee again. I continued for a whole year, realizing the entire time that it was having an unhealthy effect on me.

At the end of that year, I quit again and have remained coffee-free for another two years now. Although it still sometimes tempts me, I'm resolved to stay away from it. Doing the research for this book has probably provided the clincher for me.

I know quitting or cutting back isn't easy. It wasn't easy for me. It takes real resolve and caring strongly about your health. I wish you all the best.

Reported drug use by American adults (18 and over) for nonmedical purposes

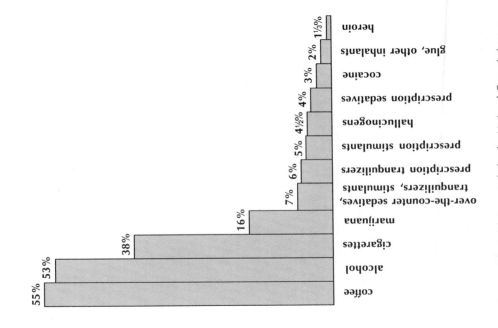

coffee — 55%
alcohol — 53%
cigarettes — 38%
marijuana — 16%
over-the-counter sedatives, tranquilizers, stimulants — 7%
prescription tranquilizers — 6%
prescription stimulants — 5%
hallucinogens — 4½%
prescription sedatives — 4%
cocaine — 3%
glue, other inhalants — 2%
heroin — 1/3%

Source: Adapted from a study by the National Commission on Marijuana and Drug Abuse. Cited in: Charles F. Wetherall, *Kicking the Coffee Habit*. Minneapolis: Wetherall Publishing Co, 1981.

Caffeine content of common foods and over-the-counter drugs (in mg)

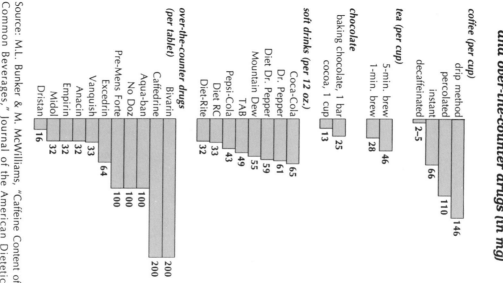

coffee (per cup)
- drip method: 146
- percolated: 110
- instant: 66
- decaffeinated: 2-5

tea (per cup)
- 5-min. brew: 46
- 1-min. brew: 28

chocolate
- baking chocolate, 1 bar: 25
- cocoa, 1 cup: 13

soft drinks (per 12 oz.)
- Coca-Cola: 65
- Dr. Pepper: 61
- Diet Dr. Pepper: 59
- Mountain Dew: 55
- TAB: 49
- Pepsi-Cola: 43
- Diet RC: 33
- Diet-Rite: 32

over-the-counter drugs (per tablet)
- Bivarin: 200
- Caffedrine: 200
- Aqua-ban: 100
- No Doz: 100
- Pre-Mens Forte: 100
- Excedrin: 64
- Vanquish: 33
- Anacin: 32
- Empirin: 32
- Midol: 32
- Dristan: 16

Source: M.L. Bunker & M. McWilliams, "Caffeine Content of Common Beverages," Journal of the American Dietetic Association, Vol. 74, pp. 28-32, January 1979. Cited in: Tom Ferguson and Joe Graedon. "Caffeine." Medical Self-Care. Winter, 1980, p.10.

Sources

See the next section, Works cited, for complete information on the works referred to in this section.

Introduction

Ferguson; Goulart/b, 1-18; Griffin; Griffiths; Tufts/c; MacMahon, 1-10; Wetherall, 18-53.

Anxiety

Bashin; Ferguson; Gilbert, 96-97; Goulart/a; Goulart/c, 12, 60, 141; Greden; Lee; LeGro; Schroepfer; Thomas/b; Wetherall, 70-71.

Asthma

Abbott; AMA/a, 119-120; AMA/b, 137-139; CMC; Clarke; Gilbert, 42, 103, 134; Graedon; Tufts/c; Pagano.

Blood pressure

Bankhead, Berkeley/a; Clarke; Edell/a; Edell/b; Ferguson; Gilbert, 77, 83-85, 101-102; Goulart/b, 12, 36, 110, 135-136; Heller, A; MacMahon, 209, 221-222; Shepherd; Wetherall, 86-88, 107-108.

Breastfeeding

Anfang; Finn; Gilbert, 78-79, 114; Hormann; Kitzinger/a, 16-32, 93-102, 151-159; Moses; Wetherall, 101-118.

Cancer

AMA/b, 175-176, 206-207, 227-229, 233; AMA/c, 616-618, 759-760, 765-767; Boyle; Brody; Ciccone; Clarke; Claude; Clavel; Goulart/b, 125-131; Heller, A; Jensen; La Vecchia/a; La Vecchia/b; La Vecchia/c; Linos; Luckmann, 439-446; MacMahon, 59-65, 109-136, 149-202; Miller; Olsen; Pozner; Rosenberg; Ross; Shepherd; Wetherall, 75-81; Whittemore.

Cholesterol

Abbott; Berkeley/c; Applegate; Bak; Curb; Davis; Gilbert, 123-124; Griffin; Shepherd; Thelle.

Pregnancy

Bashin; Brody; Caan; Pediatrics; Edell/e; Ferguson; Gilbert, 78-79, 127-132; Goulart/b, 136-137; Griffin; Heller, A.; Lecos; Martin; Salvador; Shepherd; Stern; Wetherall, 102-107.

Sleep disturbance

AMA/a,110; AMA/c, 914-916; Bashin; Clarke; Ferguson; Gilbert, 98-99, 118-119; Goulart/b, 32-33; Sorenson, 540-554; Wetherall, 66-67.

Tobacco withdrawal

AMA/c, 991-993; Benowitz; Healthline; Edell/d; Tufts/c; Tufts/b.

Vision problems

AMA/b, 430, 488-490; Carden; Davis; Higginbotham; Washington; Mindell, 125; Reuben; Sandmaier.

Vitamin and mineral loss

AMA/a, 176-179, 534-547; AMA/c, 689, 736-737, 1056-1060; Buckley; Clarke; NR; Gilbert, 104-106; Goulart/b, 22-23, 66-68, 150-152; Hamilton; Heller, L; Lally; McBean; Mindell, 3-6, 125-126, 142-144, 154, 170-172, 181-182; Munoz; Wasco.

Weight loss

Brody; Dulloo; Edell/c; Gilbert, 104-105, Goulart/b, 34-37; Hamilton; Kamimori; Kunes.

Decaffeinated coffee

Clarke; Goulart/b, 42-54; Goulart/c; MacMahon, 11-20; Okie; Berkeley/b; Willis.

Cutting back or quitting

Goulart/b, l65-188; Griffiths; Tufts/c; Wetherall, 131-134, 139-146, 160-171.

Works cited

The **boldfaced** *words below are used to identify these works in the Sources section above.*

Abbott, Peter J. "Caffeine: A Toxicological Overview." *The Medical Journal of Australia.* November 17, 1986, pp. 518–21.

AMA/a American Medical Association. *Guide to Prescription and Over-the-Counter Drugs.* New York: Random House. 1988.

AMA/b American Medical Association. *Home Medical Encyclopedia: Volume 1.* New York: Random House. 1989.

AMA/c American Medical Association. *Home Medical Encyclopedia: Volume 2.* New York: Random House. 1989.

Anfang, K. Dyanna. "Before Pregnancy: Help to Quit Cigarettes and Caffeine." *Mothering.* Summer 1987, pp. 63–68.

Applegate, Liz. "What's brewin'?" *Runner's World.* November 1989, pp. 22–25.

Aronson, David. "Coffee Gets a Break." *Men's Health.* June 1990, pp. 28–30.

Bak, A. and D. E. Grobbee. "The Effect on Serum Cholesterol Levels of Coffee Brewed by Filtering or Boiling." *New England Journal of Medicine.* November 23, 1989, pp. 1432–37.

Bankhead, Charles D. "Caffeine-Cortisol Reaction Seen." *Medical World News.* September 11, 1989, p. 21.

Bashin, Bryan Jay. "The Jolt in Java." *San Francisco Chronicle.* February 28, 1988.

Benowitz, N. L., S. M. Hall, and G. Modin. "Smoking Cessation and Plasma Caffeine Levels." *Nutrition Research Newsletter.* June 1989, pp. 64–65.

Berkeley/a "Caffeine Update: The News Is Mostly Good." *University of California, Berkeley Wellness Letter.* July 1988, pp. 4–6.

Berkeley/b "The Decaf Option." *University of California, Berkeley Wellness Letter.* July 1988, p. 5.

Berkeley/c "...and Should You Give Up Coffee?" *University of California, Berkeley Wellness Letter.* April 1990, p. 2.

Boyle, P., C. Hsieh, P. Maisonneuve, C. La Vecchia, G. MacFarlane, A. Walker, and D. Trichopoulos. "Epidemiology of Pancreas Cancer." *International Journal of Pancreatology.* December 1989, pp. 327–46.

Brody, Jane E. "Personal Health: Flurry of New Findings About Caffeine Stirs Hopes and Fears—As Well As General Confusion." *New York Times.* May 18, 1989, p. B8.

Buckley, W. T. "Bad Blood." *Redbook.* June 1989, p. 148.

Caan, B. J. and Marilyn K. Goldhaber. "Caffeinated Beverages and Low Birthweight: A Case-Control Study." *The American Journal of Public Health.* September 1989, pp. 1299–1301.

Carden, Robert. "Vitamins for Healthier Eyes." *Let's Live.* September 1984, p. 10, 12.

Carper, Jean. *The Food Pharmacy.* New York: Bantam Books. 1989.

Ciccone, G. and P. Vineis. "Coffee Drinking and Bladder Cancer." *Cancer Letters.* July 1988, pp. 45–52.

Clarke, R. J. and R. Macrae, eds. *Coffee Volume 3: Physiology.* New York: Elsevier Science Publishing Co. 1988.

Claude, J., E. Kunze, R. Frentzel-Beyme, K. Paczkowski, J. Schneider, and H. Schubert. "Life-Style and Occupational Risk Factors in Cancer of the Lower Urinary Tract." *American Journal of Epidemiology.* October 1986, pp. 578–89.

Clavel, F., E. Benhamou, A. Auquier, M. Tarayce, and R. Flamant. "Coffee, Alcohol, Smoking and Cancer of the Pancreas: A Case-Control Study." *International Journal of Cancer.* January 15, 1989, pp. 17–21.

CMC Center for Medical Consumers. "Breathing Easier...with Non-Medical Help." *Healthfacts.* April 1987, pp. 1–3.

Cohen, Sidney. "Pathogenesis of Coffee-induced Gastrointestinal Symptoms." *New England Journal of Medicine,* 1980, pp. 122–24.

Curb, J. D., D. M. Reed, J. A. Kautz, and K. Yano. "Coffee, Caffeine, and Serum Cholesterol in Japanese Men in Hawaii." *American Journal of Epidemiology.* April 1986, pp. 648–55.

Davis, B. R., J. D. Curb, N. Borhani, R. Prineas, and A. Molten. "Coffee Consumption and Serum Cholesterol in the Hypertension Detection and Follow-Up Program." *American Journal of Epidemiology.* July 1988, pp. 124–36.

Davis, R. Davis, Robert. "Does Caffeine Ingestion Affect Intraocular Pressure?" *Ophthamology.* November 1989, pp. 1681–90.

Dews, Peter B., ed. *Caffeine: Perspectives from Recent Research.* Berlin: Springer-Verlag. 1984.

Dulloo, A. G., C. A. Geissler, T. Horton, A. Collins, and D. S. Miller. "Normal Caffeine Consumption: Influence on Thermogenesis and Daily Energy Expenditure in Lean and Postobese Human Volunteers." *American Journal of Clinical Nutrition.* January 1989, pp. 44–50.

Edell/a, Dean. "Cream and Sugar, but Hold the Stress." *The Edell Health Letter.* November 1988, p. 5.

Edell/b, Dean. "Diet Pills and Coffee Don't Mix." *The Edell Health Letter.* January 1989, p. 3.

Edell/c, Dean. "Skip the Coffee Diet." *The Edell Health Letter.* May 1989, p. 1.

Edell/d, Dean. "Ex-smokers High on Caffeine." *The Edell Health Letter.* August 1989, p. 5.

Edell/e, Dean. "Coffee and Diabetes." *The Edell Health Letter.* June/July 1990, p. 3.

Eisig, J. N., S. Zaterka, H. K. Massuda, and A. Bettarello. "Coffee Drinking in Patients with Duodenal Ulcer and a Control Population." *Scandinavian Journal of Gastroenterology.* September 1989, pp. 796–99.

Fabro, S. and S. M. Sieber. "Caffeine and Nicotine Penetrate the Preimplantation Blastocyst." *Nature.* 1969:223, pp. 410–12.

Faelten, Sharon. "Putting on Heirs: New Treatments for Male Infertility." *Men's Health.* Fall 1987, pp. 78–82.

Ferguson, Tom and Joe Graedon. "Caffeine." *Medical Self-Care.* Winter 1980, pp. 8–12.

Finn, Susan Calvert. "The Caffeine Question." *American Baby.* March 1989, pp. 32–34.

Fishman, Ricky. "Natural Headache Cures." *Medical Selfcare.* November/December 1989, pp. 24–29, 64.

Gilbert, Richard. "Caffeine: The Most Popular Stimulant." *The Encyclopedia of Psychoactive Drugs.* New York: Chelsea House Publishers. 1986.

Goulart/a, Frances. "Caffeine: The Legal Addiction." *Whole Life Times.* December 1983, pp. 20–22.

Goulart/b, Frances. *The Caffeine Book: A User's and Abuser's Guide.* New York: Dodd, Mead and Company. 1984.

Goulart/c, Frances and Junu Bryan Kim. "In Search of the Perfect Decaf: Are You Substituting Chemicals for Caffeine?" *Bestways.* November 1989, pp. 45–48.

Graboys, T. B., C. M. Blatt, and B. Lown. "Caffeine and Arrhythmias." *Nutrition Research Newsletter.* May 1989, p. 52.

Graedon, Joe and Teresa. "Self-Care for Asthma." *Medical SelfCare.* July/August 1987, p. 16.

Greden, J. F. "Anxiety or Caffeinism: A Diagnostic Dilemma." *American Journal of Psychiatry.* 1974:131, pp. 1089–92.

Greif, Judith. "All About Headaches." *New York.* March 9, 1987, pp. 57–64.

Griffin, Katherine. "Good News for Java Junkies." *Hippocrates.* December 1989, pp. 18–21.

Griffiths, R. R., G. E. Bigelow, and I. A. Liebson. "Human Coffee Drinking: Reinforcing and Physical Dependence Producing Effects of Caffeine." *Journal of Pharmacology and Experimental Therapeutics.* November 1986, pp. 416–25.

Grobbee, Diederick and E. Rimm, E. Giovannucci, G. Colditz, M. Stampfer and W. Willet. "Coffee, Caffeine and Cardiovascular Disease in Men." *New England Journal of Medicine.* October 11, 1990, pp. 1026–32.

Hamilton, Kim. "The Weight-Loss Perk: Caffeine's Kick May Help Keep Excess Pounds in Check." *Health.* July 1989, pp. 32–34.

Hammond, Mary and Luther Talbert, ed. *Infertility: A Practical Guide for the Physician.* New Jersey: Medical Economics Co. 1985.

Healthline "Caffeine May Increase Withdrawal Symptoms." *Healthline.* October 1989, p. 5.

Heller, Arthur. "Caffeine Controversy Brewing: Is It Worth the Perk?" *Shape.* September 1987, pp. 58–61.

Heller, L., L. J. "Keep Your Bones Straight and Strong." *Redbook.* March 1989, p. 22.

Higginbotham, Eve, Heidi Kilimanjaro, Jacob Wilensky, Randal Batenhorst, and David Herman. "The Effect of Caffeine on Intraocular Pressure in Glaucoma Patients." *Ophthalmology.* May 1989, pp. 624–26.

Hormann, Elizabeth. "New Breastfeeding Challenges." *Mothering.* Fall 1989, pp. 66–70.

Jensen, O., J. Wahrendorf, J. Knudsen, and B. Sorensen. "The Copenhagen Case-Control Study of Bladder Cancer. II. Effect of Coffee and Other Beverages." *International Journal of Cancer.* May 15, 1986, pp. 651–57.

Joesoef, M. Riduan, V. Beral, Robert Rolfs, Sevgi Aral, and Daniel Cramer. "Are Caffeinated Beverages Risk Factors for Delayed Conception?" *Lancet.* January 20, 1990, pp. 136–37.

Kaminori, Gary. "Caffeine Effects on Exercise and Fat Loss." *Shape.* September 1987, p. 60.

Kitts, D. "Studies on the Estrogenic Activity of a Coffee Extract." *Journal of Toxicology and Environmental Health.* 1987:20, pp. 37–49.

Kitzinger/a, Sheila. *The Experience of Breastfeeding.* New York: Penguin Books. 1980.

Kitzinger/b, Sheila. *The Complete Book of Pregnancy and Childbirth.* New York: Alfred A. Knopf, Inc. 1983.

Klapper, J. A. "The Treatment of Acute Migraine Headaches." *Headache Quarterly, Current Treatment and Research.* 1991, Volume 2, No. 1, pp. 83–89.

Kunes, Ellen. "The New Diet Buzzword—Caffeine!" *Mademoiselle.* October 1989, p. 230.

Lally, S. "Knock Out Fatigue with the 'Iron Fist'." *Prevention*. November 1988, pp. 55–59.

Lance, James W. *Migraine and Other Headaches*. New York: Charles Scribner's Sons. 1986.

Lark, Susan. *Premenstrual Syndrome Self-Help Book*. Los Angeles: Forman Publishing, Inc. 1984.

La Vecchia/a, C., R. Talamini, A. Decarli, S. Franceschi, F. Parazzini, and G. Tognoni. "Coffee Consumption and the Risk of Breast Cancer." *Surgery*. September 1986, pp. 477–81.

La Vecchia/b, C., P. Liati, A. Decarli, E. Negri, and S. Franceschi. "Coffee Consumption and Risk of Pancreatic Cancer." *International Journal of Cancer*. September 15, 1987, pp. 309-13.

La Vecchia/c, C., M. Ferraroni, E. Negri, B. D'Avanzo, A. Decarli, F. Levi, and S. Franceschi. "Coffee Consumption and Digestive Tract Cancers." *Cancer Research*. February 15, 1989, pp. 1049–51.

Lecos, Chris. "Caffeine Jitters: Some Safety Questions Remain." *FDA Consumer* (HHS Publication No. (FDA) 88-2221. Department of Health & Human Services). December 1987/January 1988.

Lee, Bill. "Caffeine's Nerve Stimulation Can Help Sports Performance: Endurance and Alertness Promoted, but as Many as 20 Percent May React Badly." *Health News & Review*. March/April 1988, p. 6.

Lee, M. A., P. Flegel, J. F. Greden, and O. G. Cameron. "Anxiogenic Effects of Caffeine on Panic and Depressed Patients." *American Journal of Psychiatry*. May 1988, pp. 632–36.

Legro, B. "When Panic Strikes...Don't Panic." *Prevention*. April 1989, pp. 112–13.

Liebmann-Smith, Joan. "Does Stress, Smoking or Bacteria Really Cause Ulcers?" *Self*. February 1990, pp. 170–74.

Linos, A., D. A. Linos, N. Vgotza, A. Souvatzoglou, and D. Koutras. "Does Coffee Consumption Protect Against Thyroid Disease?" *Acta Chirurgica Scandinavica*. June/July 1989, pp. 317–20.

Luckmann, Joan and Karen C. Sorensen. *Basic Nursing: A Psychophysiologic Approach*. Philadelphia: W. B. Saunders Company, pp. 438–553. 1979.

McBean, L. D. "Calcium Sources: Some Considerations." *Dairy Council Digest*. May/June 1989, pp. 13–17.

MacMahon, Brian and Sugimara Takashi, Ed. *Coffee and Health* (Banbury Reports Series Volume 17). Cold Spring Harbor, NY: Cold Spring Harbor Laboratory, 1984.

Marshburn, P. and C. Sloan, M. Hammond. "Semen Quality and Association with Coffee Drinking, Cigarette Smoking and Ethanol Consumption." *Fertility and Sterility*. July 1989, pp. 162–65.

Martin, Terry R. and Michael B. Bracken. "The Association Between Low Birth Weight and Caffeine Consumption During Pregnancy." *American Journal of Epidemiology*. 1987:126, pp. 813–21.

Miller, D. R., L. Rosenberg, D. Kaufman, S. Helmrich, D. Schottenfeld, J. Lewis, P. Stolley, N. Rosenshein, and S. Shapiro. "Epithelial Ocarian Cancer and Coffee Drinking." *International Journal of Epidemiology*. March 1987, pp. 13–17.

Mindell, Earl. *Shaping Up with Vitamins*. New York: Warner Books. 1985.

Moses, Lenette S. "Drugs and Breastmilk." *Mothering*. Summer 1990, pp. 68–73.

Munoz, L. M., B. Lonnderdal, C. L. Keen, and K. G. Dewey. "Coffee Consumption as a Factor in Iron Deficiency Anemia Among Pregnant Women and Their Infants in Cost Rica." *American Journal of Clinical Nutrition*. September 1988, pp. 645–51.

Napier, Kristine. "Exercise Fact and Fallacy." *Mature Health*. October 1989, p. 20.

NIH National Institutes of Health. *Headache, Hope Through Research*. Maryland: September 1984, NIH Publication No. 84–158.

NR "Dietary Caffeine and Calcium Excretion." *Nutrition Reviews*. June 1988, pp. 232–34.

NRN/a "Caffeine and Competitive Sport: How Much Is Too Much?" *Nutrition Research Newsletter.* January 1989, p. 11.

NRN/b "Caffeine and Decreased Fertility." *Nutrition Research Newsletter.* February 1989, p. 17.

NRN/c "Effects of Caffeine on Platelet Function." *Nutrition Research Newsletter.* February 1989, p. 22.

Okie, Susan. "Decaffeinating Coffee Without the Chemicals." *San Francisco Chronicle.* August 28, 1987.

Olsen, G., J. Mandel, R. Gibson, L. Wattenberg, and L. Schuman. "A Case-control Study of Pancreatic Cancer and Cigarettes, Alcohol, Coffee and Diet." *American Journal of Public Health.* August 1989, pp. 1016–19.

Pagano, R., E. Negri, A. Decarli, and C. La Vecchia. "Coffee Drinking and Prevalence of Bronchial Asthma." *Chest.* August 1984, pp. 386–89.

Pediatrics "Caffeine and Your Unborn Baby." *Pediatrics for Parents.* June 1989, p. 5.

Pozner, J., A. Paptestas, R. Fagerstrom, I. Schwartz, J. Saevitz, M. Feinberg, and A. Aufses, Jr. "Association of Tumor Differentiation with Caffeine and Coffee Intake in Women with Breast Cancer." *Surgery.* September 1986, pp. 482–88.

PT "Premenstrual Syndrome: The Caffeine Connection." *Psychology Today.* June 1989, p. 13.

Rakel, Robert E., Editor. *Conn's Current Therapy 1991.* Philadelphia: W. B. Saunders Company. 1991.

Reuben, Carolyn. "Diet and Vision." *L. A. Weekly.* August 25–31, 1989.

Rivkin, Jacqueline. "A Cup of Infertility?" *American Health: Fitness of Body and Mind.* June 1989, p. 124.

Rosenberg, L., M. Werler, J. Palmer, D. Kaufman, M. Warshauer, P. Stolley, and S. Shapiro. "The Risks of Cancers of the Colon and Rectum in Relation to Coffee Consumption." *American Journal of Epidemiology.* November 1989, pp. 895–903.

Ross, R., A. Paganini-Hill, J. Landolph, V. Cerkins, and B. Henderson. "Analgesics, Cigarette Smoking, and Other Risk Factors for Cancer of the Renal Pelvis and Ureter." *Cancer Research.* February 15, 1989, pp. 1045–48.

Rossignol, Annette M., Jianji Zhang, Yongzhou Chen, and Zheng Xiang. "Tea and Premenstrual Syndrome in the People's Republic of China." *The American Journal of Public Health.* January 1989, pp. 67–70.

Russell, L. C. "Caffeine Restriction as Initial Treatment for Breast Pain." *Nurse Practitioner.* February 1989, pp. 36–39.

Salvador, H. S. and B. J. Koos. "Effects of Regular and Decaffeinated Coffee on Fetal Breathing and Heart Rate." *American Journal of Obstetrics and Gynecology.* May 1989, pp. 1043–47.

Sandmaier, Marian. "Decaffeinate and See Straight." *Mademoiselle.* March 1989, p. 146.

Schroepfer, Lisa. "Panic by the Cupful: Dropping Caffeine Can Sometimes Cure a Severe Anxiety Disorder." *American Health: Fitness of Body and Mind.* June 1989, p. 46.

Shepherd, Steven. "Caffeine and Health: The Latest On the World's Most Popular Drug." *Executive Health Report.* May 1989, p. 7.

Sims, Thomas J. "Headaches in Women: Management Strategies." *The Female Patient.* May 1991, p. 36.

Solomon, Seymour and Steven Fraccaro. *The Headache Book.* New York: Consumer Reports Books, 1991.

Sorenson, Karen and Joan Luckmann. *Basic Nursing: A Psychophysiologic Approach.* Philadelphia: W. B. Saunders, 1979.

Stamford, Bryant. "Caffeine and Athletes." *The Physician and Sportsmedicine.* January 1989, pp. 193–195.

Stern, Judith. "Your Diet: Caffeine Update." *Vogue.* February 1988, p. 430.

Theile, D. S., S. Heyden, and J. G. Fodor. "Coffee and Cholesterol in Epidemiological and Experimental Studies." *Atherosclerosis.* October 1987, pp. 97–103.

Thomas/a, P. "Bad Sperm Role Emerging in Birth Defects, Infertility." *Medical World News.* October 14, 1988, p. 38.

Thomas/b, P. "An Anxious Age." *Medical World News,* January 9, 1989, pp. 34–36, 39–40, 43.

Troiano, Linda. "A Cuppa Trouble? New Study Strengthens Link Between Caffeine and PMS." *American Health: Fitness of Body and Mind.* October 1989, p. 40.

Tufts/a "Caffeine Suspected in Impaired Fertility." *Tufts University Diet and Nutrition Newsletter.* April 1989, p. 2.

Tufts/b "Trying to Quit Smoking? Drink Less Coffee." *Tufts University Diet and Nutrition Letter.* November 1989, p. 1.

Tufts/c "Grounds for Breaking the Coffee Habit?" *Tufts University Nutrition Letter.* February 1990, pp. 3–6.

Ward, N. and C. Whitney, D. Avery and D. Dunner. "The Analgesic Effects of Caffeine in Headache." *Pain.* February 1991, pp. 151–55.

Wasco, J. "Osteoporosis: Taking Calcium May Not Be Enough." *Woman's Day.* September 13, 1988, p. 14.

Washington "Keeping an Eye on Caffeine." *Washington Post.* November 29, 1988, p. 18, col. 1.

West, Susan. "The Hell in My Head." *Hippocrates.* May/June 1987, pp. 33–44.

Wetherall, Charles F. *Kicking the Coffee Habit.* Minneapolis: Wetherall Publishing Company. 1981.

Whittemore, A., M. Wu, R. Paffenberger, Jr., D. Sarles, J. Kampert, S. Grosser, D. Jung, S. Ballon, and M. Hendrickson. "Personal and Environmental Characteristics Related to Epithelial Ovarian Cancer. II. Exposures to Talcum Powder, Tobacco, Alcohol, and Coffee." *American Journal of Epidemiology.* December 1988, pp. 1228–40.

Wilcox, Allen, Clarice Weinberg, and Donna Baird. "Caffeinated Beverages and Decreased Fertility." *Lancet.* December 1988, pp. 1453–55.

Williams, J. H. "Caffeine and Exercise Performance." *Nutrition Research Newsletter.* May 1989, pp. 51–53.

Willis, L. R. "Caffeine Debate Goes On." *San Francisco Chronicle.* August 26, 1987.

Other books from Odonian Press

The Decline and Fall of the American Empire
Gore Vidal

Vidal is one of our most important—and wittiest—social critics. This little book is the perfect introduction to his political views.

What Uncle Sam Really Wants
Noam Chomsky

A brilliant analysis of the real motivations behind US foreign policy, from one of America's most popular speakers. Full of astonishing information.

Burma: The Next Killing Fields?
Alan Clements

If we don't do something about Burma, it will become another Cambodia. Written by one of the few Westerners ever to have lived there, this book describes the current nightmare vividly.

Who Killed JFK?
Carl Oglesby

This brief but fact-filled book gives you the inside story on the most famous crime of this century. You won't be able to put it down.

They're available at most good bookstores, or send $5 per book + $2 shipping per order (not per book) to Odonian Press, Box 7776, Berkeley CA 94707. Please write for information on quantity discounts, or call us at 510 524 3143